AF600817

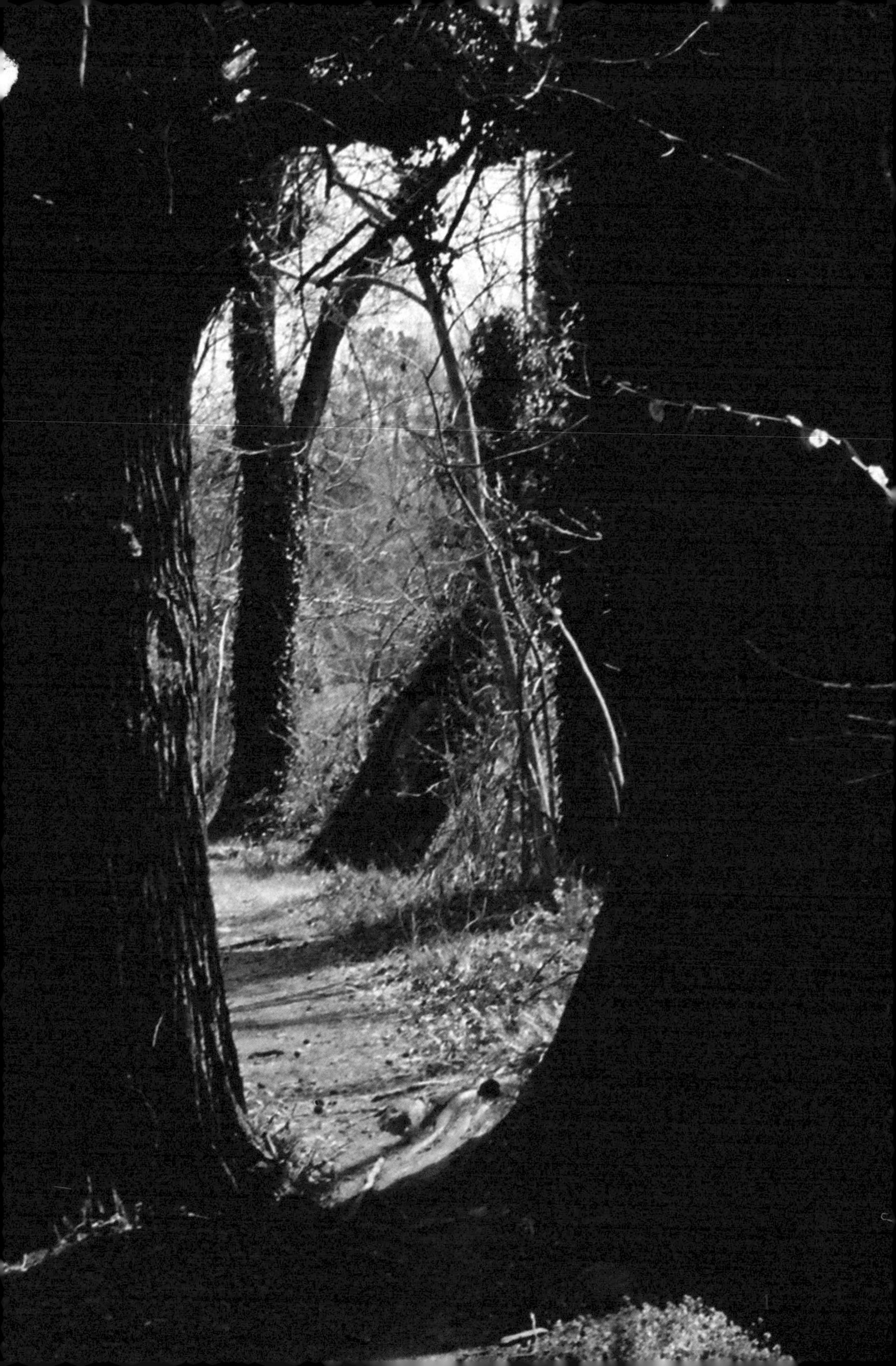

HUNTERS FOLLOW HARPY SHADOWS

RIN KIM

Contents

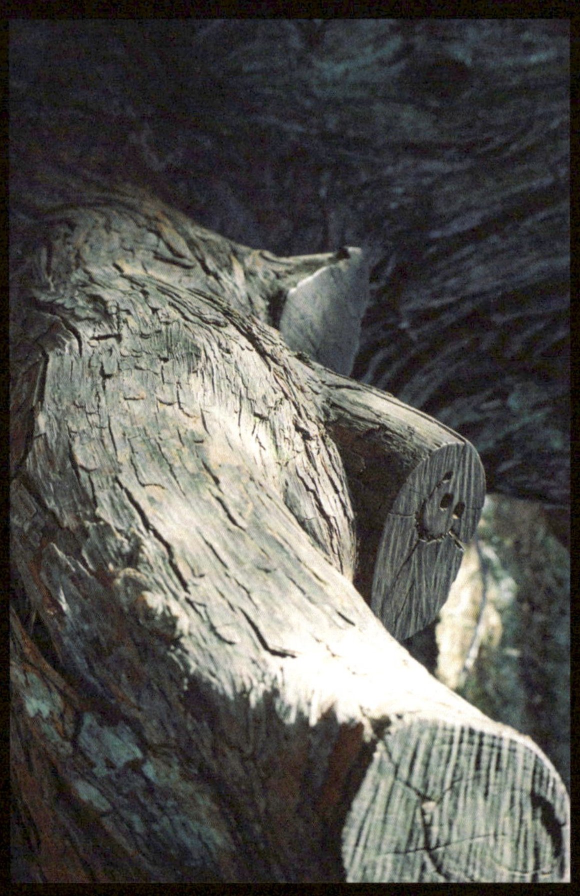

OLD TESTAMENT

of the Snow

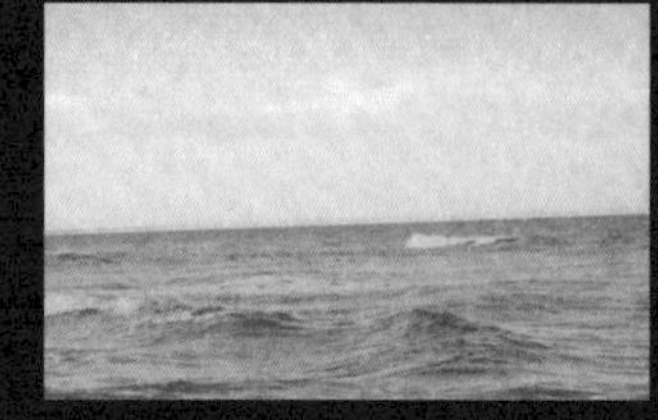

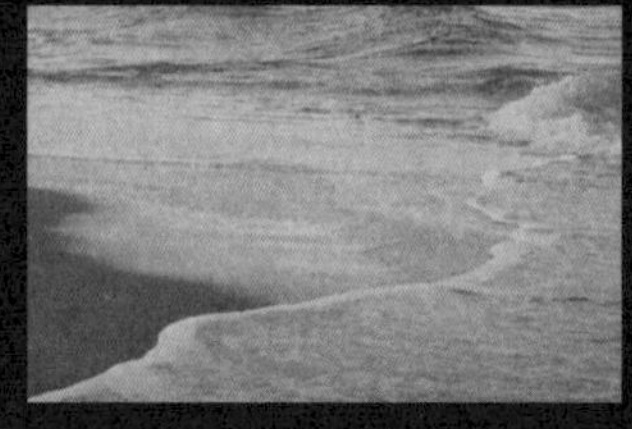

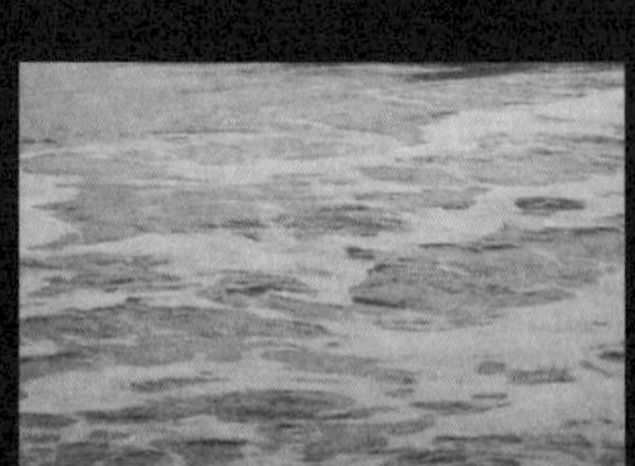

During the origins of the earth, mortals sacrificed their children to the belly of the depths, to Yawong: god of subservience and singularity. In this time Soo Yeil, child of the south, was taken by her parents to the temple of earth and water as sacrifice to show the god their faithfulness. As Soo Yeil sank to the bottom of the sea, her soul was gently pulled from her body and hidden in the belly of an oyster. When Yawong came to feast, he found the frame was void.

In his fury, he cast his seal upon the body, a seal of lightning and scales, making the body swear that if Soo Yeil's soul ever returned, it was the right of Yawong to claim it. But over the next 400 years, Soo Yeil's soul began to learn many things of itself and in the soft body of the oyster, began to change and grow new flesh. The soul formed a new body made of pearl and steel, finally getting so large that it burst forth. Soo Yeil hunted down their original frame and freed the wretch by baptizing it in pomegranate juice.

This body then gave itself to Soo Yeil, knowing its time had come and gone, and was burned to ashes and scattered over the earth. The ashes were of pure white, like starlight, from the purifying and cooled from the baptism in sweet icy nectar. The mortals called it snow and it covered the earth. Soo Yeil, now free in his new body transmuted and transfigured by its own desires and freedoms, was blessed by the goddex of fertility, Keida, a goddex of both father, mother, healer. Xe gave him the gift of divinity, making him the new god of the sea. Xir unborn lion serpent child that watched from xir womb, Deoe, blessed Soo Yeil with the sword of Aracia, the two-tongued blade that could split heaven.

With these gifts, Soo Yeil took to the sea to find Yawong feasting on the children of mortals and split the god into nine pearls which were placed in the belly of Nuwa, the third sun with many eyes.

GODS DO NOT PRAY

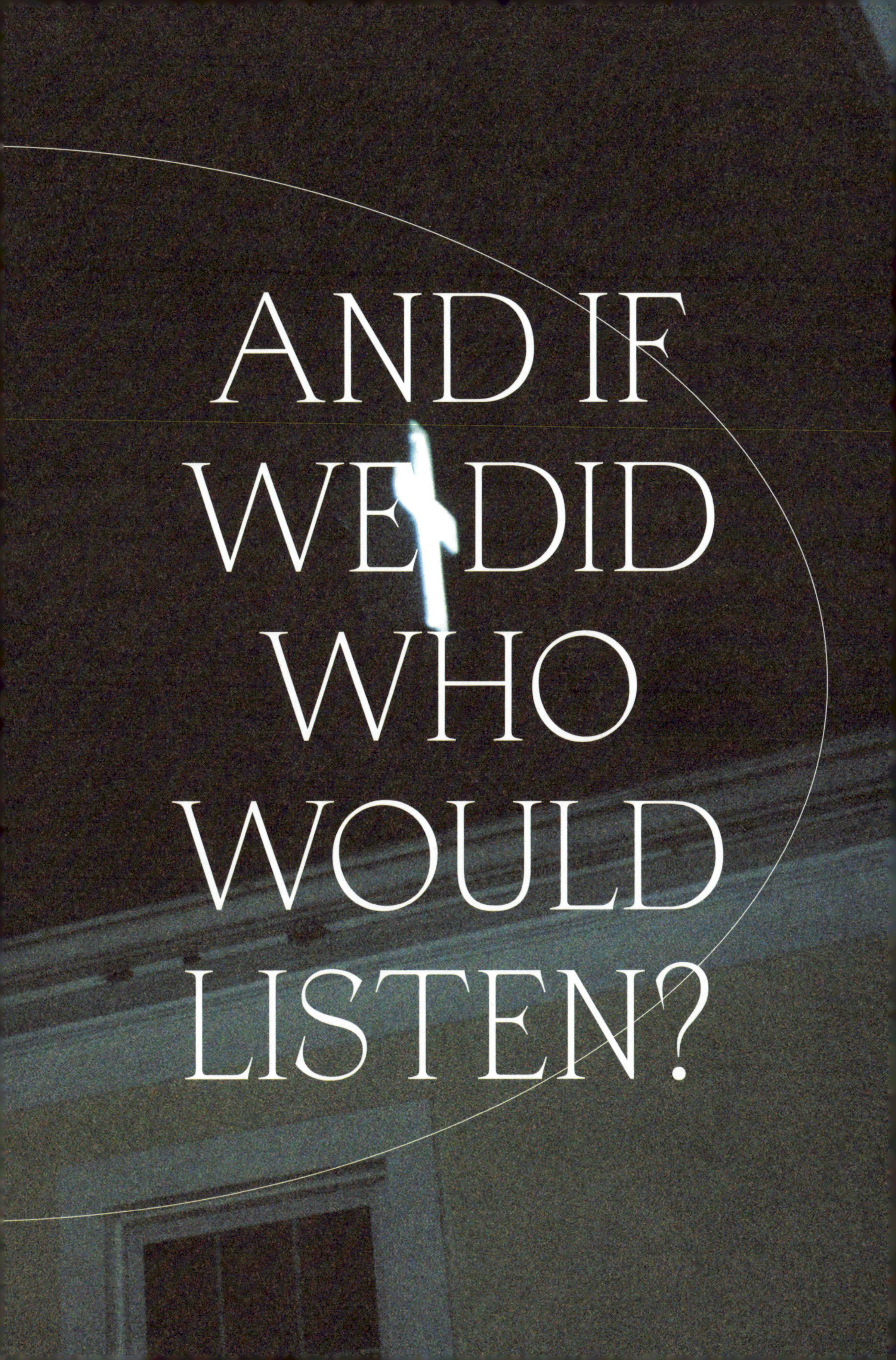

AND IF
WE DID
WHO
WOULD
LISTEN?

PSALM OF SOO YEIL

To darkness I am given and to darkness I return.
And the song that immortals hear – I can almost touch it.
Smooth string of pearls I swallow until my body becomes the forge.
And through the womb of vengeance
I am remade by her grace and suspended.
And to you my body; come to me my love.
I set the dinner table as I always have
I get you water, you always ask for more
No explanation for I understand thirst
But that isn't what this is
And I consume myself
All flesh and fluid
I bathe in lemon juice and those anointed
with my blessings pour wine over my lips
You have never apologized

And in the quiet spaces when I passed from death unto life
I remember you
And I still love you, as I love myself now
I have never loved a past self, and in pity and regret
I apologize to her. I apologize over and over and over
enough times to make up for the thousands of apologies
she has missed, or if she had left the house a little earlier
might have heard before going.
And I consume myself.
With only the gods to bear witness

I fear you will tell them of what I was before I became myself
That you will give me as your offering once again
That you will get caught in the selfishness
of your sentiments once again
That I will lose you once again

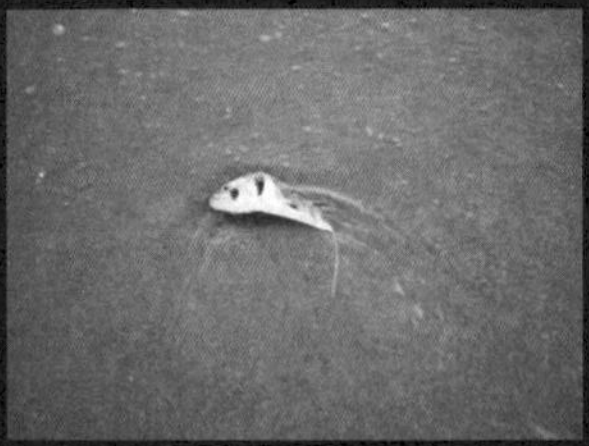

Gods do not pray.
And if we did, who would listen to our prayers?
My body is given to me, and I pass through holy fire
with my fate left to my own powers.

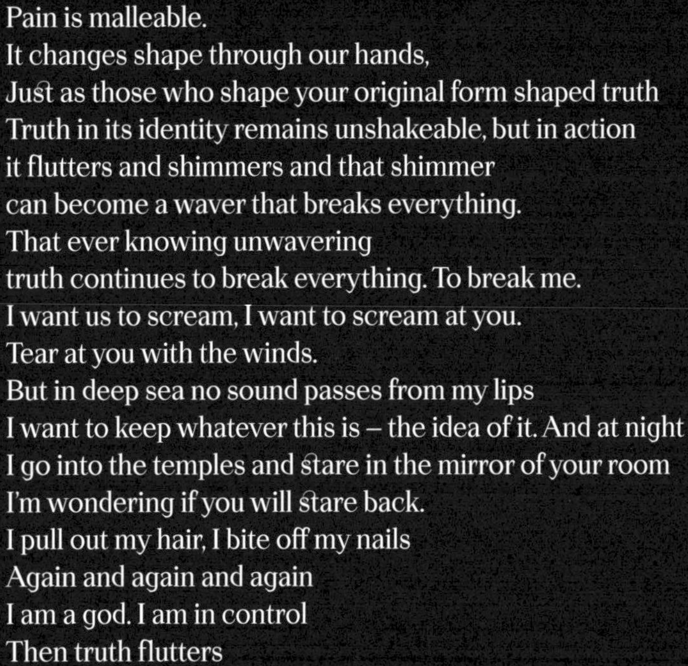

Pain is malleable.
It changes shape through our hands,
Just as those who shape your original form shaped truth
Truth in its identity remains unshakeable, but in action
it flutters and shimmers and that shimmer
can become a waver that breaks everything.
That ever knowing unwavering
truth continues to break everything. To break me.
I want us to scream, I want to scream at you.
Tear at you with the winds.
But in deep sea no sound passes from my lips
I want to keep whatever this is – the idea of it. And at night
I go into the temples and stare in the mirror of your room
I'm wondering if you will stare back.
I pull out my hair, I bite off my nails
Again and again and again
I am a god. I am in control
Then truth flutters

And when I throw up it's the scream.
My mouth is open and I am silent.
I am brought back to the depths of the ocean.
I am made empty.
I am left bare.

And who do I pray to now?
Demi. With heart of a mortal. Mind of a god.
I am here for you. To hear your prayer.
And I will carry you home.
I will carry myself home.
To my name. To my body.
To darkness you are given.
And it is darkness that will hold you.
And to darkness we will return.

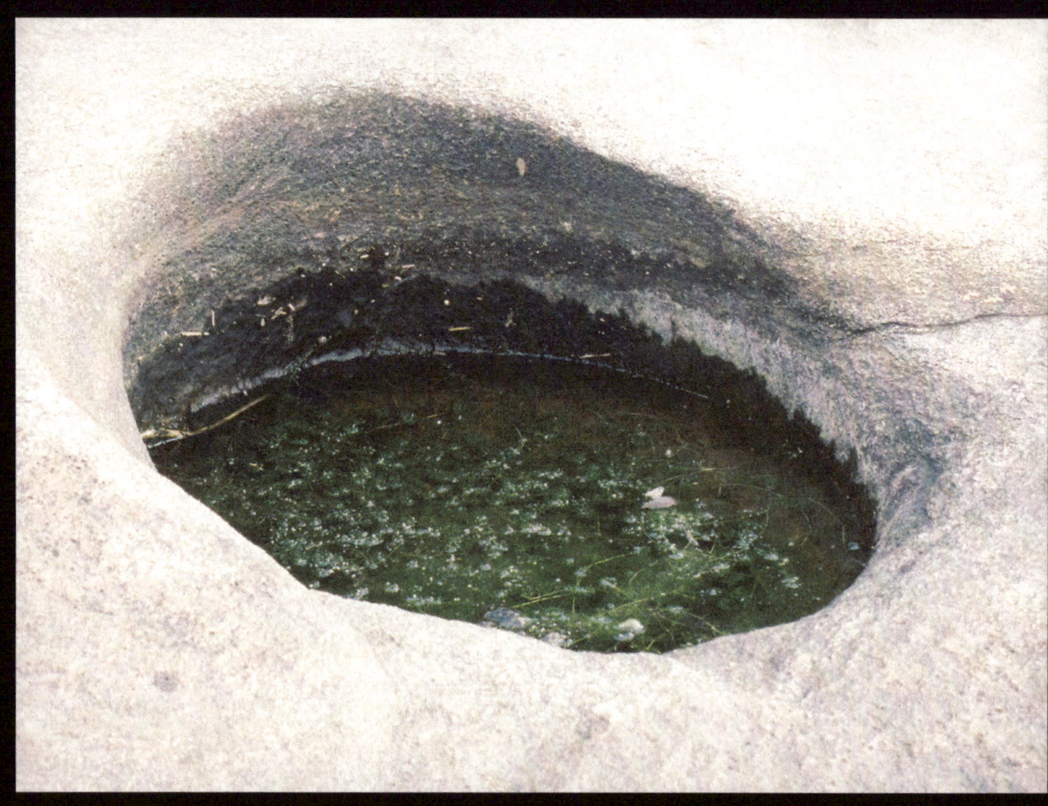

Chu'shi'ien and Vlkiri, the twin planets that orbit around the sun. Each planet with all mortal spirits split in two, getting the chance to live different lives on each. One day, the spirit inhabiting one planet will realize where its destiny truly belongs and will break out of its mortal frame and fly as fast as it can to make itself whole on the other world. With it bringing the devastation of all past memories, while celebrating being once again whole. Long before they chased themself around the sun, they were one spirit Chi'Vir. In this form, they made a pact with the wolf god, Nau, for they loved him deeply. Each night, they would watch him swallow the sun and keep it safe in his belly until morning, his eyes burning with fire and sacred bindings.

And they watched this from the fields of the universe in awe and aching and longing as love blossomed and took root in and around the beast of heaven. And the two fell deep and far into one another's futures and pasts, intertwining their bodies and longings. But as it was written in deep magic, Nau had to go to the dragons of the southern seas and have them ferry the sun from his belly before morning. Otherwise, the sky would crack and wail with despair, bringing all the universe to darkness. And Chi'Vir was tasked with playing the harp, which lulled all beasts and deities to deep slumber, to keep them from waking and stumbling into oblivion in the darkness. But Chi'Vir would leave their post once an hour or so had passed and go to Nau, for they could only meet in a sky of total darkness, always trusting the other would come into the pitch black, when other gods and beasts stayed in their beds for safety.

But one night Chi'Vir became lost in the darkness, unable to find Nau. And Nau waited too long and the sun began to burn his belly and he had to leave to allow it to rise. Aracia, the old god of the universe (who the two-tongued blade which could split heaven was named of), who was neither merciful nor cruel, had to deal with the affairs of his son Nau (born of the werewolf Nakti). Aracia split his son Nau partly into the sun and partly to create a moon to become companion to the sun and placed all the planets between them so there would never be true darkness again. He then split Chi'Vir into two.

Chu'shi'ien (the song that lays waste to the riverbed) became the planet that lulled the heavens to sleep, and Vlkiri (the passion of two suns) was charged with ensuring all loves for all history would be able to find one another set to orbit the sun. Aracia then decreed that whenever Vlkiri and Chu'shi'ien caught one another, all the heavens would stand still and the moon and sun would once again form Nau, and Vlkiri and Chu'shi'ien would form Chi'Vir, and for one hundred years time would stop and they could be together.

I'LL DEVOUR YOU. SPIT YOUR BONES OUT INTO THE DUST

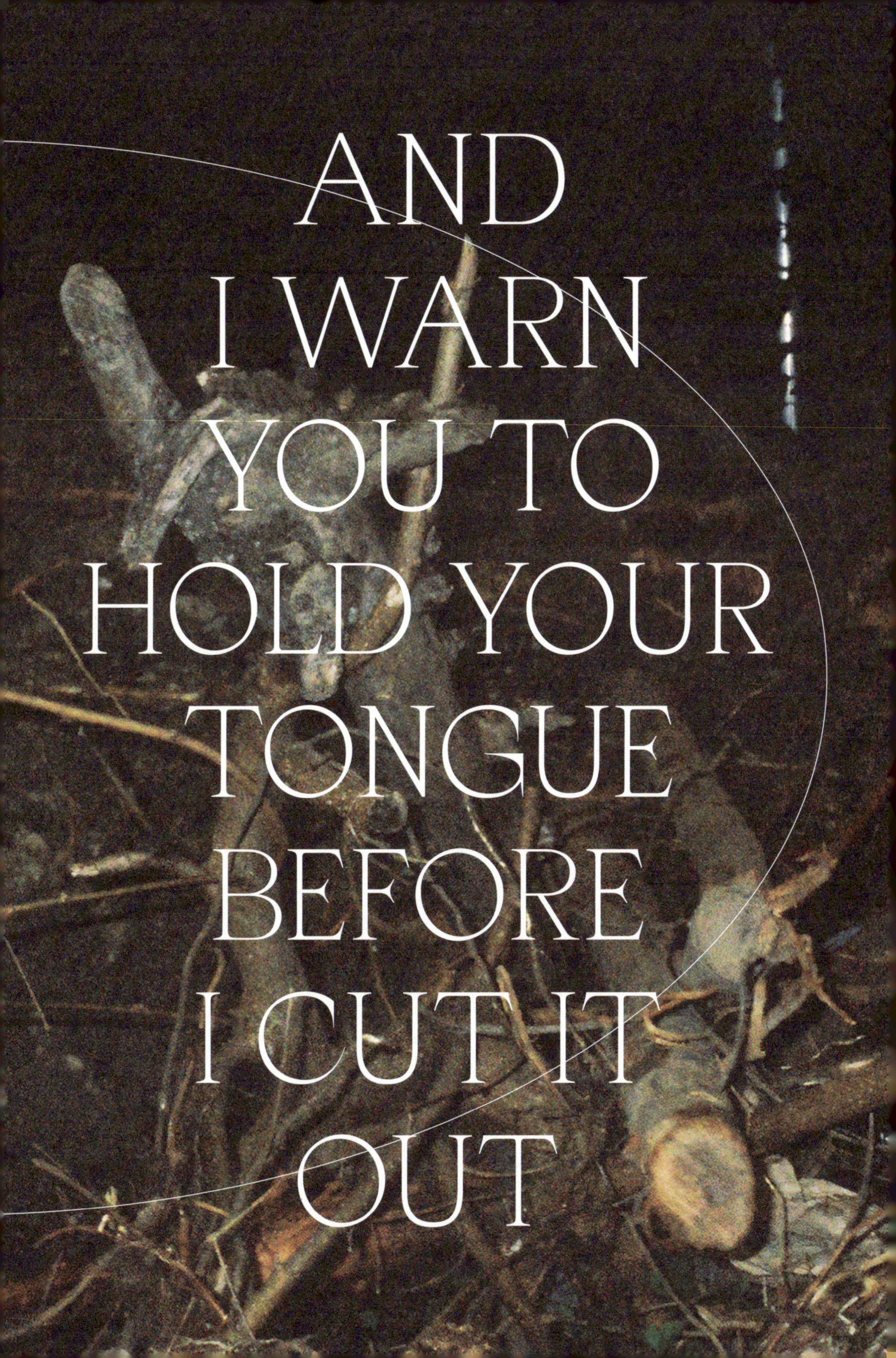

AND
I WARN
YOU TO
HOLD YOUR
TONGUE
BEFORE
I CUT IT
OUT

PSALM OF HERESY

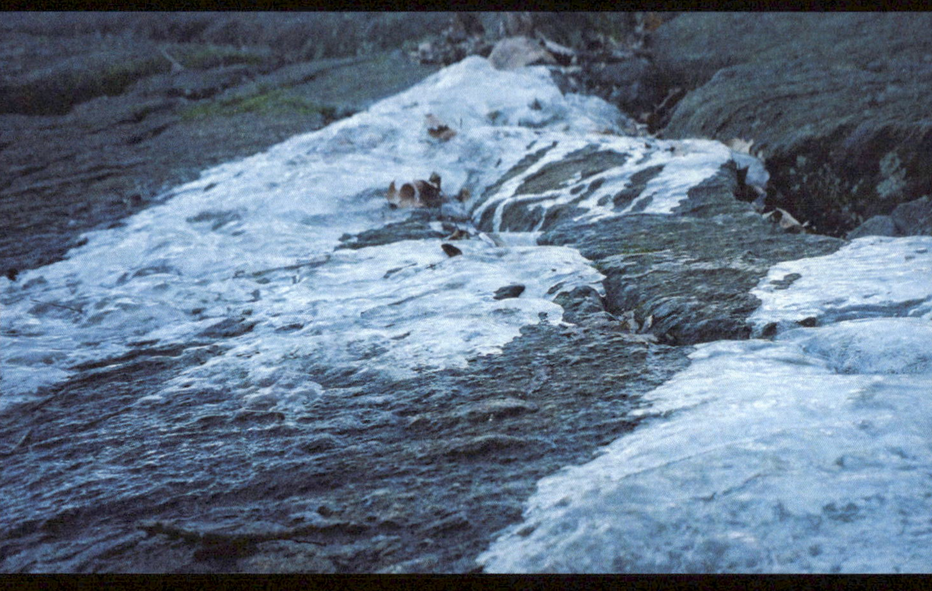

You come to my land – a place so dark god can't even see

They burn me alive and the fire wraps around my legs like
the yong woven into my people's temples, like the veins in my own

They ask me to stay silent as they stitch my skull back together
I do. Without complaint
They feed me strawberries for holding back my tears,
now pain tastes like them

I wrap myself in care
My womb empty, made for
me in constant rebirth.
I lose myself and I lose you baby
I lose myself and I lose you
I try to hold you in my body
I try to hold you in my arms
In embrace I crush myself

I try to hold you in my arms
In embrace I crush myself

Fire is my lover and it fucks me in the dark
Fire is my penance and it takes me without allegiances
What they wrote in the finalities: renewal / Hamlet telling
of his father's wrath: rewrote as a myth to encompass:
it was he who killed him

(act one) slit his throat like a fawn (tender) held in the arms
of love (revenge)

I am held in the arms of love. And as I return they refute my desire.
They spit it out and I bathe in it like rice wine
that begins to boil at the touch
The ocean boils at my touch

 It resists touch
 It transcends touch

Not to trust lineage or blood though it resides
at the inner wall of your defenses

"Catch for us the foxes, the little foxes who ruin our gardens,
our gardens that are in bloom"

Rewritten like those who herald death, famine, the hunger of the King
withering on the throne,
the spirits you call to you are purged
with a life force leaving the anointed

Baptize me in lambic wine
so the flies devour me
Holy sweetness
When I am nothing I will
return to my spirit

I'll devour you
Spit your bones out into the dust
And I warn you to hold your tongue before I cut it out.

The King's Head

Before the ships of Yazuko came from the palace of heaven, three infernal kings ruled hell at the time after the fog of terra. The king of shame, Shal'eiva; the king of despair, Herahd; and the king of disease (of the body, mind, and soul), Yomgae.

They were brothers, born out of the single egg of a phoenix. Shal'eiva had a daughter with the great minotaur Ei'Kein. Herahd, a son with the river serpent Vi, and Yomgae gave birth to a child with the black hole who came to earth in the body of a Pegasus, Yamada. The three kings were charged by hell to protect the free lands from the emperor of the western lands, Maru (who mortals called the jackal's scepter). Maru was a bloody tyrant and had violently conquered the celestial shimmer and the elves that had dwelled there since the dawn of times.

The kings of hell waged war upon Maru, hoping to right the imbalances of the kingdoms. Through ritual sacrifice, Maru formed his daughter Ryiah (she who was made from molten earth). Maru worshipped Jrhivah (who all living things trembled before). Maru gave his elf wife's soul in return for Ryiah and she was baptized in lava to become impenetrable by any blade made on earth.

It was Ryiah who was appointed his general. Carrying out the unspeakable. That which the bards, mages, and historians of her world refused to chronicle. It was Ryiah who, also in the second era of Maru's dynasty, was released from their father's curse. Her mind was opened and made new by the goddess of mercy. Ryiah was renamed by the goddess: Erolas (in old tongue, the right hand of the divine). Erolas, to atone for his crimes, offered up his right arm to the temple of Sephiroth, god of atonement and victory, bartering for the return of the souls of those he'd slaughtered.

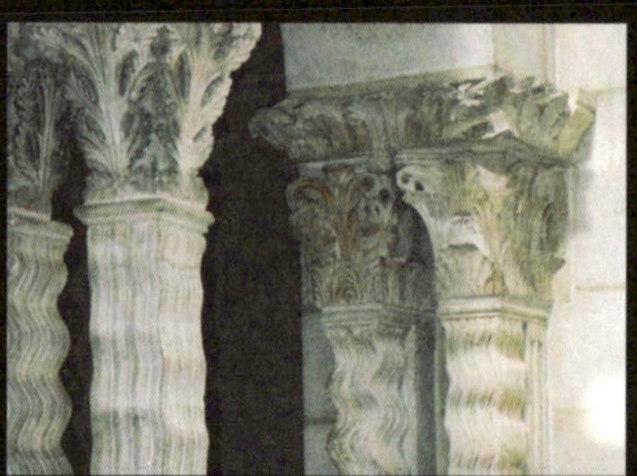

Sephiroth, though known as one who did not often listen to the prayers of earth, listened to Erolas, for the god had watched what the half-elf had done and was shocked his soul could be re-made at all. The dead rose anew. And Erolas brought himself for atonement at the feet of the kings of hell. They struck a bargain: if Erolas led their armies, killed his father, and then gave his whole body as blood sacrifice to Naslela (dragon of the eastern keep) they would accept his rebirth.

Erolas and Kyzah, Yomgae's son, led the last of the free armies against Maru (many historians report that the two men were lovers, and in their next reincarnation found one another and were reincarnated as the two dragons who circled the keep of Vane). And it was Erolas who beheaded Maru on the battlefield in Sylvin territory, a field that would later be renamed Nav-rii (the place where the earth is bone), ending Maru's reign. Erolas then gave his body to the infernal kings to be sacrificed, much to the despair of Kyzah, and all lands were once again free and the children of hell returned to hell and the elves reclaimed their lands.

The spirit worlds released all who had died in the name of Maru and Erolas's body was devoured by the hounds of hell who ferried back their souls.

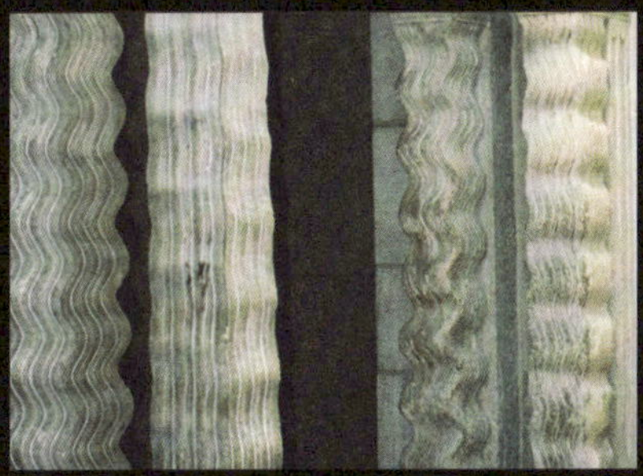

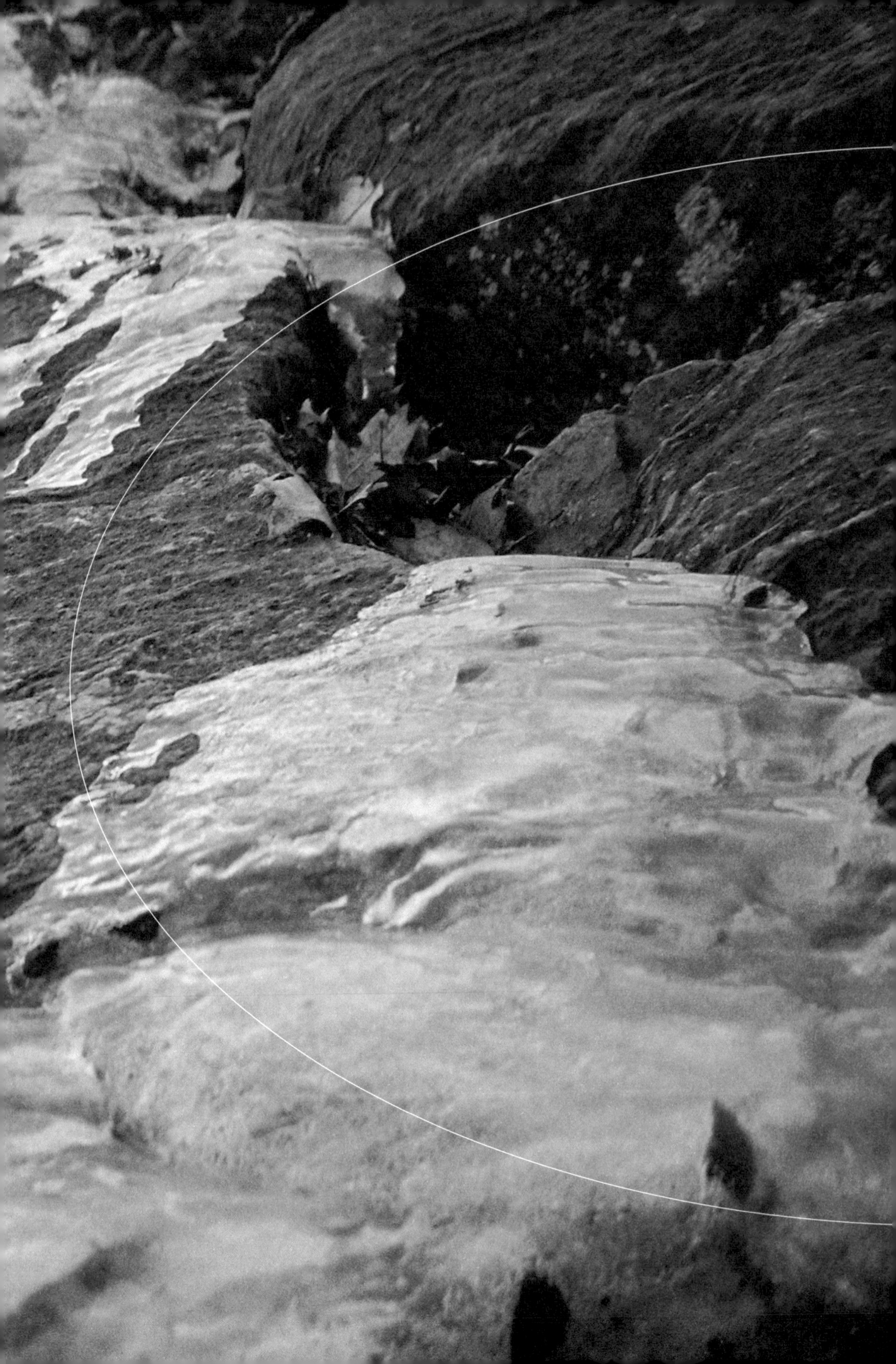

AND NOW MY SURNAME, DESERTER, IS MELDED TO ME

PSALM OF EROLAS

It is my father who sends me to war.
And it is I who die for his name.
His name which is drenched in bile and
said with the bitterness of those
who now rot in the mud.

When I place leeches, they take his blood
from me and I cook them in rosemary,
hibiscus, sesame oil, and white pepper.
I serve them to him and he eats his sons
like the gods of the old world.

The court watches him perish.
His blood as poisonous as he left it in me,
his last son and it takes from him
what it has taken from me.
He is a sacrifice to the ancestors of
the blood that remains running to the
finish line.

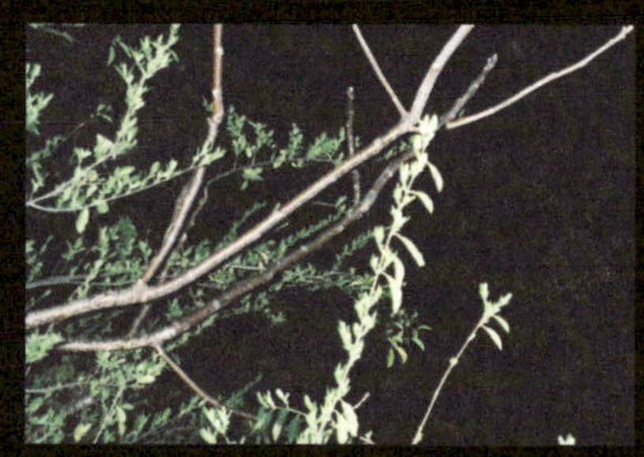

They choose the stake for treason.
It is my father who beckons me to war
and it is I who was born to tread the path
of blood.

And now my surname,
deserter, is melded to me

:: I am unbound.
Unfurled by this evil.
It tangles within me and I draw it like a
silk between my forearms.

: daughter of a daughter of farmers. One
who has seen through ten thousand eyes.
Of a people who see through the mind
of resistance, I beseech you: leave this
shadow to consume another.

Did they not cross the sea
for abundance?

: to dethrone whatever blood has been given, I shake heavy wings to take me from this place. What hath come before the steps of gods to assume I would not learn to live in the belly of the serpent?

He devours the world and I
in turn am nourished in the dark

Tell me lord of this place,
why do you draw me from
its splendor?

: When you spit teeth and black bile comes from your bowels, you will understand. When your children curse your name far from where they have buried your legs and head.

They bury your liver in the sea and your heart in the wilderness. Your eyes burned to ash and are rubbed into the floor of the temple. Your daughters will die. This is what I have foretold at the pool of the world.

I foretell the youngest will be born a lamb and from the ribs of the lamb a wolf in its clothing. Its muscles ripple with indigo and the cost will grow long in the summer. He will travel to the ends of the map and there be cast away from Valhalla.

He will break all oaths,
take on his father's ring

This is what I foretell
at the pool of the world

: and these sacred promises you make
come from clear water
: the pool is as dark as blood and rich as milk. The line once corrupted stays and there is no second chance to the chances we take on love. You will perish with only your eldest by your bedside and that will be the last of your father's line.

Your youngest son in his despair will sink his claws into ghosts but his body will become a tomb for your memories that can never be reclaimed. This is what you have done at the end of the race. A legacy for becoming nothing more than your own mother.

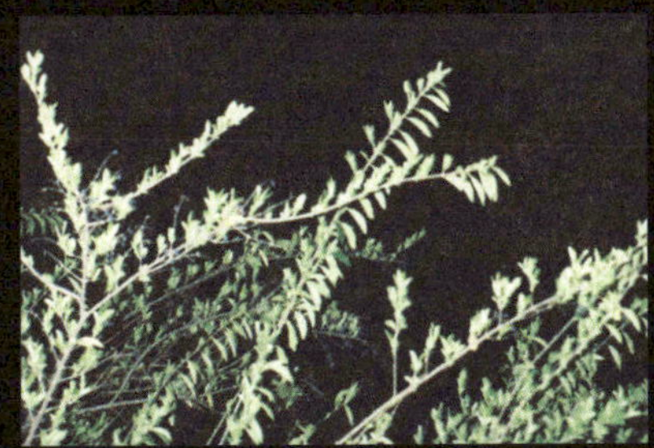

Host Body

On the outskirts of the second coordinate galaxy, 4.00.59 beta 6, the bards sang of ships who would wander too close to the anomaly of the holy sea, where spirits of felled behemoths would jump into the bodies of crew members. Lethe, a behemoth, was the titan of stealth (a half werewolf mer child of Loki). Lethe jumped from the lunar rivers into the body of the pirate Sorel. Lethe had been wandering the channels of the afterlife and began to despair in their new host body.

They allowed Sorel's consciousness to return to their mind and they convened together; the beast and the mortal. Lethe eventually went mad; their body, which used to be of such beastly might – such a magnificent casing for their spirit – now wilted in a mortal frame.

Their soul fractured into two parts, their natures gone rampant and eventually they were taken by madness and consumed. Sorel, who was blessed by the goddex Reya, whose followers were the archers of the new world, was spared by their patron deity, and Lethe in their weakened form was exorcised. Sorel was tasked with returning their spirit to the holy sea, where Lethe's mind was once again made anew and their soul reformed.

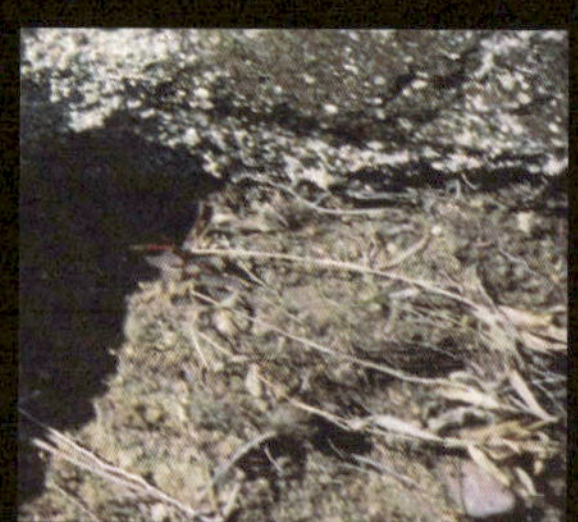

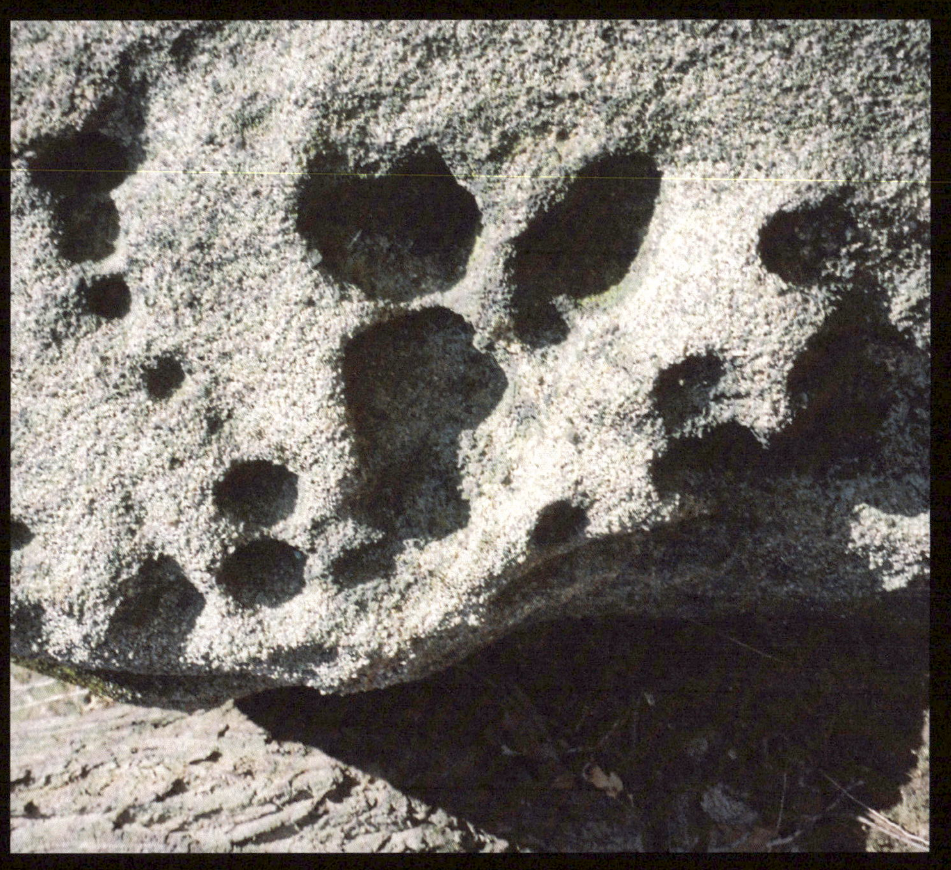

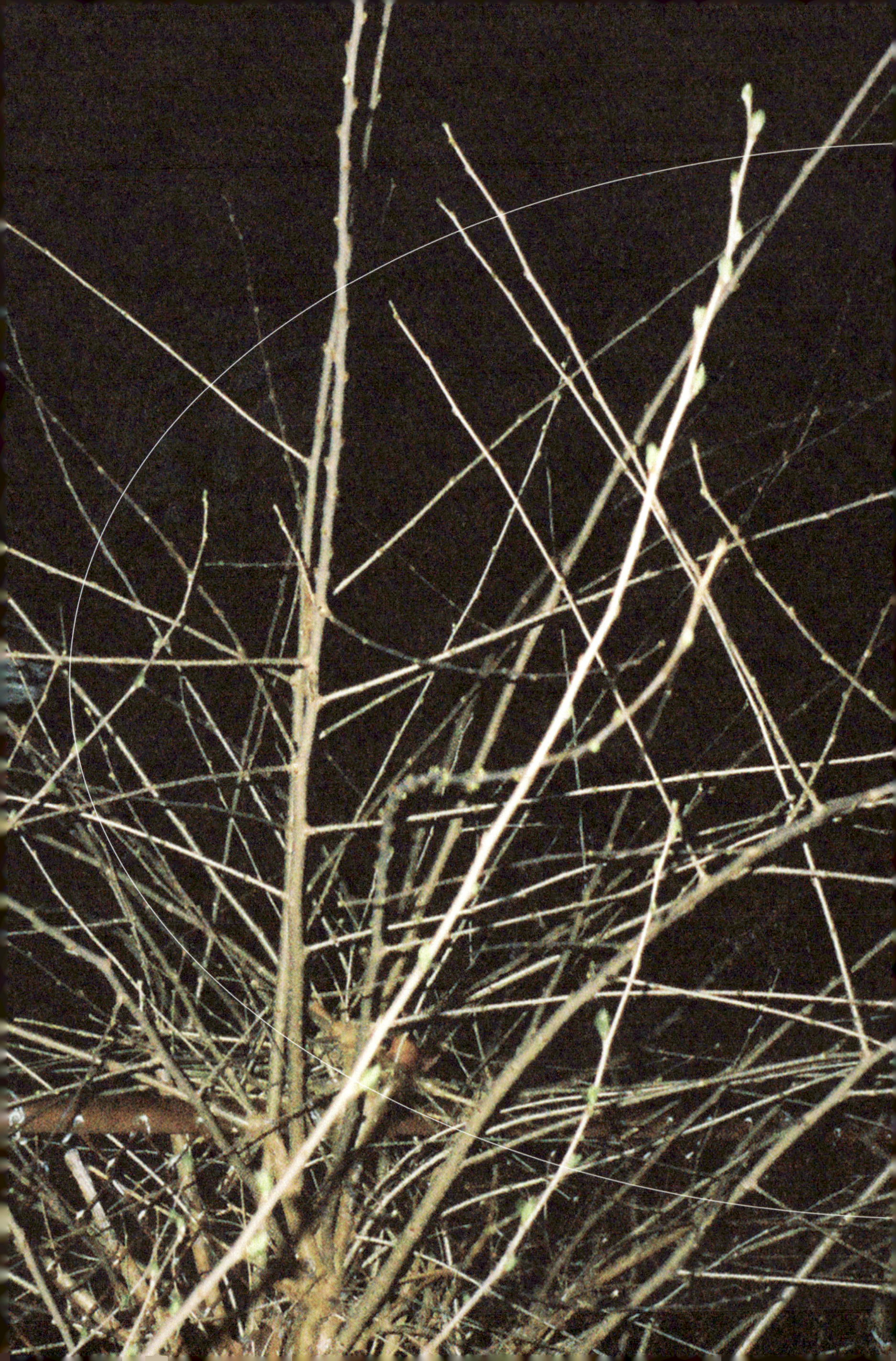

I WATCH
MY VEINS
BEGIN TO
MOVE AND
SLITHER UNDER
THE SKIN OF
MY HANDS.
THIS WAS
THE PATH
OF DESIRE

We share this body of mine.
As the paradox of pleasure and ownership you own this house just as much as I own myself and I am and you exist here as I live and breathe I am a temple, silent. My body exists to renew my absolute existence, but now as a ghost I wander the earth absolved of definitive being. Tracks in the snow, I follow you out into space where I am forlorn.

I sit in the host body of a woman, how I feast upon human flesh.
In many myths they see my identity as twofold, a bolt unravels to unveil
I am the lover, regaining my body through that of fucking my lover.
They want to see me as tender, a vessel to be filled, made with loneliness desiring transient escape. But as we fold the other side to this story of violence: feasting on the bodies of the unwilling.

I wonder what part of identity is based on mythic truth and how willing is the audience to change the story when I change? Can I change and remain the same as I was? May I feast on mortal flesh yet remain as I am, I desire blood but I don't need to change to be fulfilled. I am complete. In my never solid form I am complete.

They tell ghosts to become man again or to vanish. The ghost as bridge, never destination. Why must my destiny be wrought with becomings?

I ask the gods to send a sign
I watch my veins begin to move and slither
under the skin of my hands
This was the path of desire

You mirror me.
Cheap imitation like melting back into the earth.
Like leather melting into my hands in the heat.
Steam burns under the feet of the leopard,
I massage his hands while the light grows old.
Older than I have ever seen,
in past lives and the one after this,
it persists and resists death
though she creates many paths to run to her.

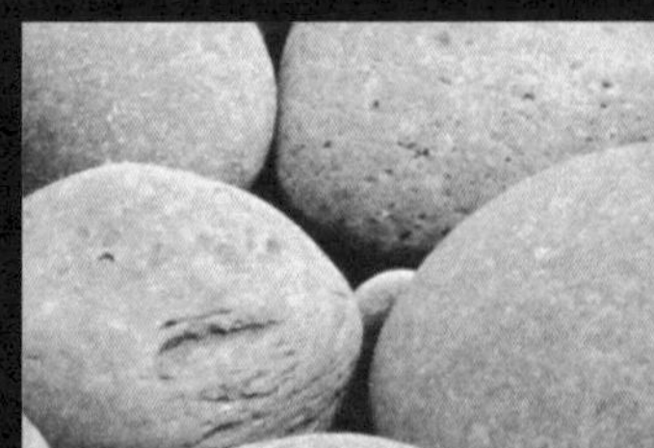

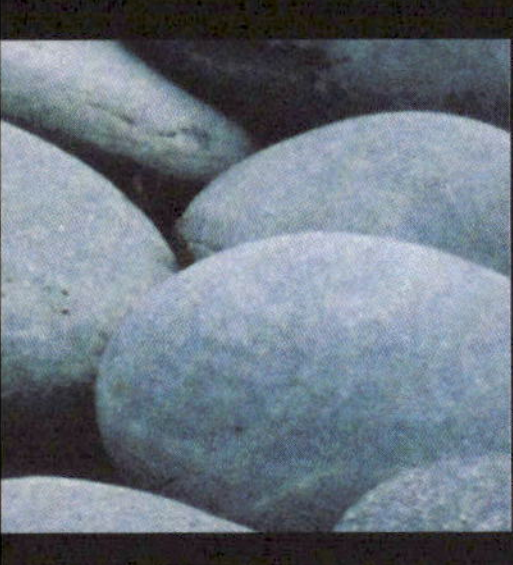

If the sun were to rise indigo,
if my body were to be borne by the winds east
if my kin were to be blessed with knowledge
would I then understand the parts
of myself that were never formed in riverbeds and hot rain?

Sleep, seated on the throne
Hearing the whispers of your sons
A king is alone with blood and wine and the cries of his people
No man should rule alone.

Insatiable hunger, moth who drinks the tears of the horse
I leave my lover to become the jackal,
ripe is the flesh on my mortal frame,
draft wind, I feel the knife but I see not your hands.
You mirror me, tears of the horse become the bathhouse at night.
Steam from hot springs mask a weeping willow whose branches
shackle me to this place. You say stay. My back pulses and aches,
the muscles remember flight before the gods snatched it from me
I ache for power. To go far from you.
My hands shake and quiver under the bow causing the arrow
to miss its mark.
The arrow leaves its mother and with no marking
it claims a new creator.
Object of new origin in the claiming of a new heaven.

Your hands that hold a thousand suns
And orbiting those suns five thousand ships
The fleet of heaven that bore every breed of star
Where the children of Reya, woman man and father of malice
bore his children, the Inuil.

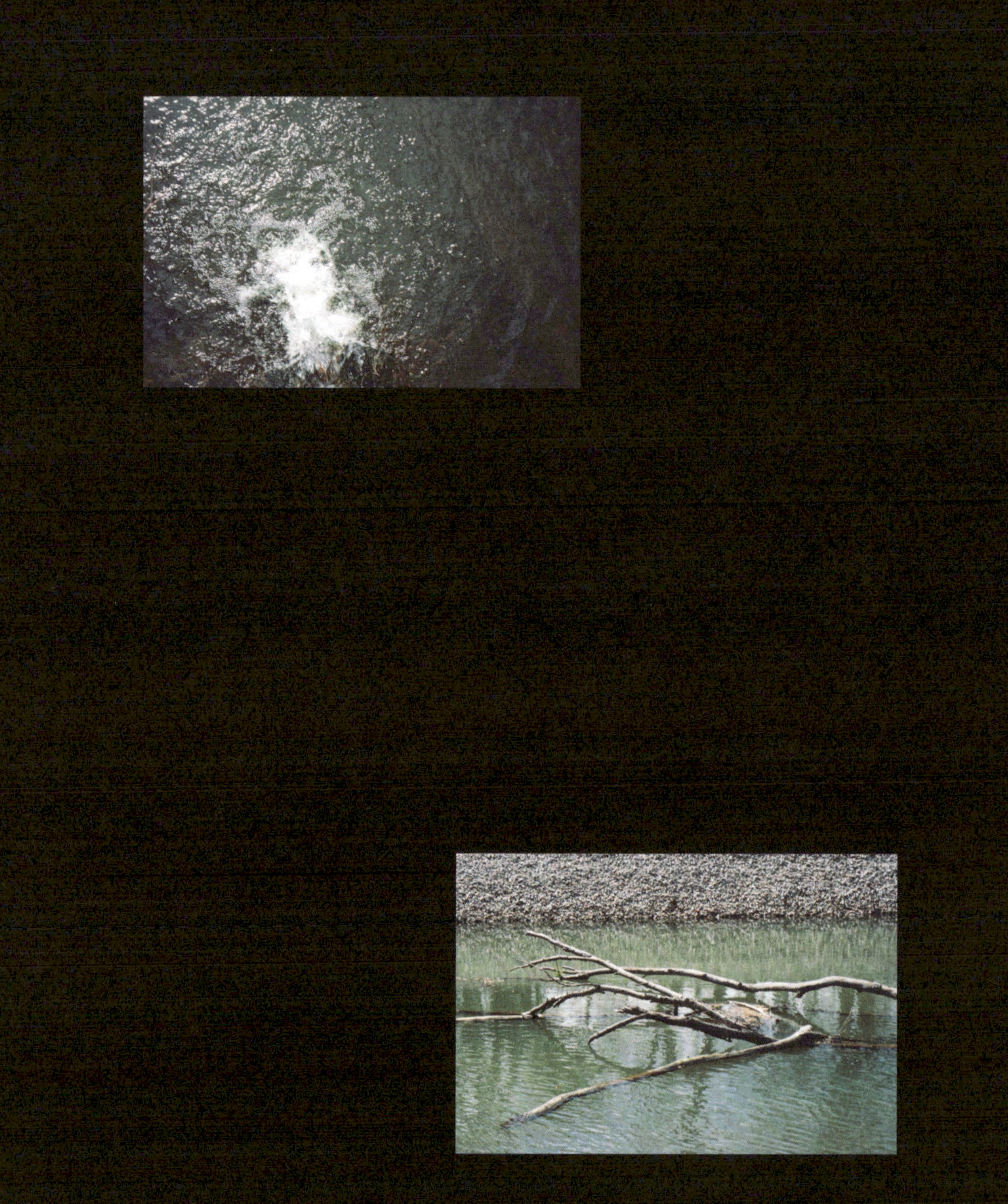

They say that Anevhe was the deity of the voiceless scream. Of the sound that leaves the lips of those in despair when their tears prohibit speech. The same sound that howls over an endless body of water. That leaves the lips of the gull far from home. Anevhe, who was the grandchild of the untameable. Their anger deeper and wider than heaven. For like the mist, their sentiments waned and waxed over many eons. The lesser gods took vengeance upon Anevhe unjustly. They cast them to the Pits of Vakk'tu, the place where the light does not shine and the mud pulls those slowly deeper into her stomach. Three times was Anevhe destroyed and reborn. Their body rotting away, hair falling out, fangs slipping from their mouth to the mud and three times their spirit renewed itself, reforming flesh from within. The desire to exist perseveres in every fog. You hear those at rock bottom cry to Anevhe, those with no roads left to turn to. Their prayers are answered with the gentleness found not in holiness, but in rage.

Anevhe, who appeared to sailors as a blue fog, was cousin to Calypso, the wild tidal wave and thunderclap in the blackness of the night who is only found when their hair blots out the stars. Found in the fast song, by the fires burning on the pirate ships of Agmire. Of the drums that beat around them, Calypso is the liquor that flows over open water. For as Anevhe hides the crestfallen from their kin's retribution (none of heavy heart may drown under the blue fog) with the forgiveness found in those who see eye to eye, Calypso is protector of the reveler and criminal. All pirates pray to be under the protection of the god Calypso of chaos. Those are the two laws of the sea. Calypso, the champion of the sinner, and Anevhe, the protector of the heavy of heart – and the sea sings her song to both. Calypso, the sea, Anevhe, the winds that rush over it.

The devil makes a deal with Calypso,
The desperate pray to Anevhe.
Thus is the nature of the twin tongues that defy heaven.

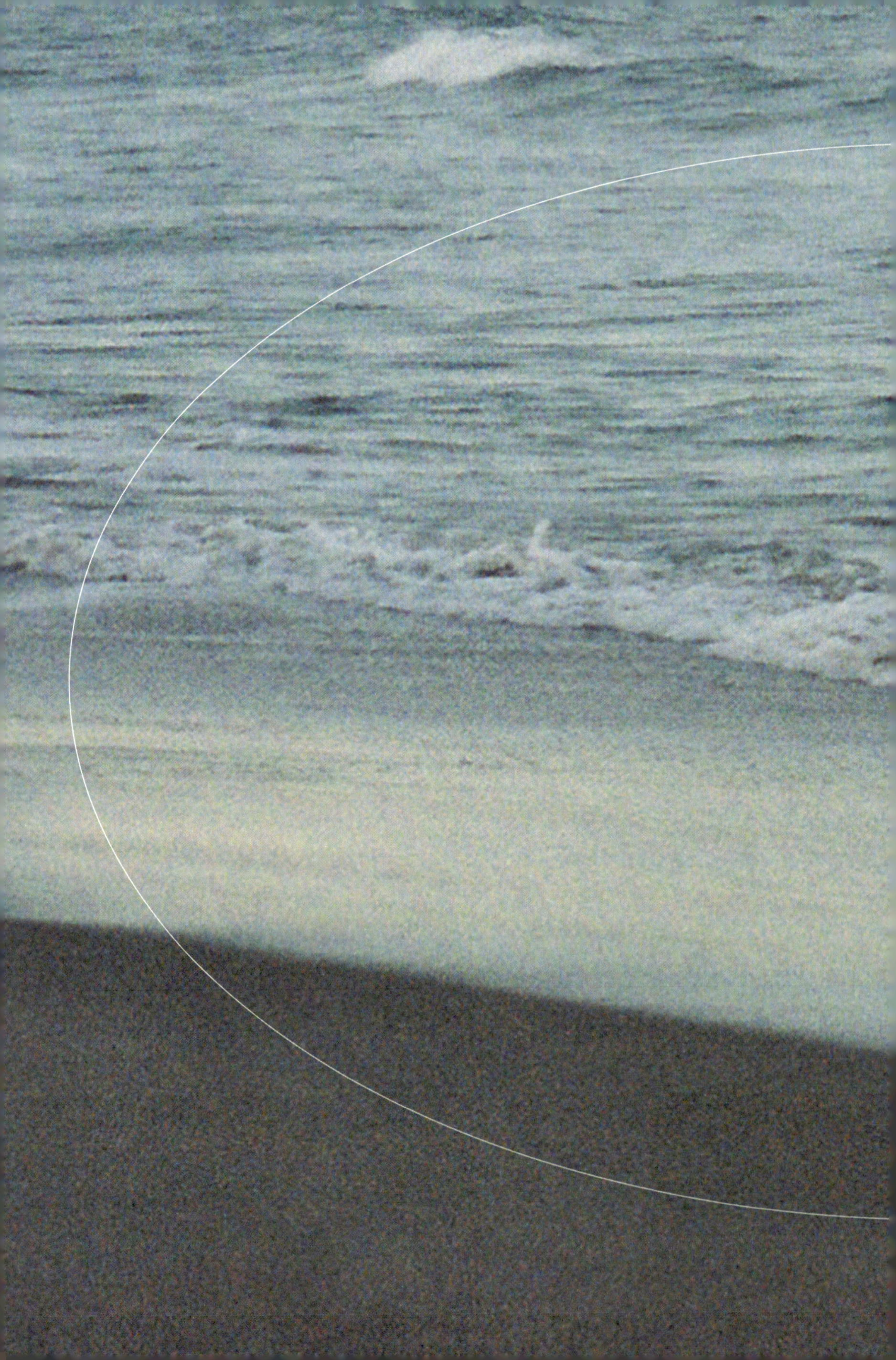

WATER
ACHES
WITH
US

PSALM OF CALYPSO

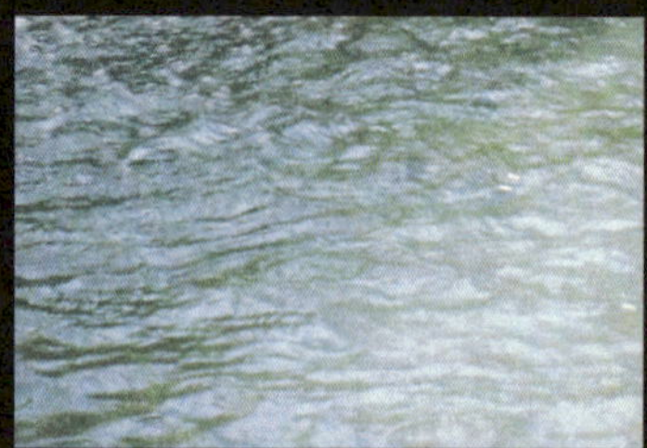

She who comes across the sea.
Her tears are the salt of the earth.
Her bones are unbreakable.
Unmatchable.

She who is the crash
and the thunder
The electricity that runs through
the skin of mortals

For the strong do not fear death,
but know there is worse
than death waiting
in the hearts of men.

And I am taken to the ends of the earth
to hear my kin Calypso's wailing.
I hear it in the beasts of our land and
the scream that comes when words
cannot follow weeping.

A hawk leaves three slits
down your arms and I hold
the skin to keep you from
bleeding out
A boy ties his brethren to
the mast and holds the ropes
between his tendons when Eer'yki,
goddess of storms, trembles.

White-knuckled, crushed salt, the night
that falls over the sea where land
becomes memory
is the virtue of bad men.

Where the dexterous
show their quality.

She is undefeated and unmastered.
For the thought of another woman
she becomes weak-kneed at love,
a woman who is unravelled
is powerful in her desires.

A woman who is wholly destined for
herself as well as the elements which
govern her sentiments.

All sailors carry weighted dice
All deities of the sea hold court
for the crazed and forsaken
The madman is baptized in saltwater,
emerging red-eyed and hot to the touch
Flesh like iron, spit like steel

The siren knows all yearning,
in the throbbing and
quivering the siren sees
the unfulfilled aching of the mortal
and calls them to open water.

Water aches with us.
The ocean hungers and swallows ships
to the darkness
She thirsts and swallows the light
whole, the sanity of those thought
the heartiest among us.
This itching burning needing
the ocean does know.

Great river that flows
swiftly to the sea, all waters
which are drawn by her.

Many lovers in a house
made of willow trees, in the shade
of the ocean fowl's wings.

Watched carefully by lightning
and held fast by many spirits
who stay close to our earth
to pay tribute to she who they
cannot cast from their mind.

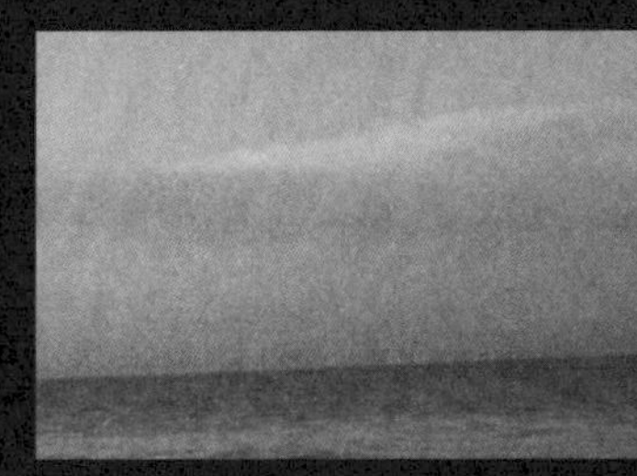

Dream of a Sailor on Her Sea

Joon Soo was flung from heaven and where he landed was the front seat of a car with a baby on his lap, a cigarette resting in his smile. They said he was proud because he was a driver, and the children of his children find solace at the wheel.

His lover Calypso flew across the sea, leaving her beloved and child to the new world. His back pressed to the seat of the car, feeling the two wounds where god ripped his wings from his body. Parlay as a prayer as he crosses the sea, baby in his lap, the Sword of Damocles sheathed in embroidered silk.

> But I wake up and this was all a dream. I wake up with my back pressed against the deck of the ship. Like my brother's hand on a hot stove, I gasp for air wondering if in the dream I was drowning? If I was burning? The water is too much. I hear it crash on the hull, crash like my body when it hit the water?

My heart is racing and as my hands splinter and follow the rhythm of necessity – the blood rushes and feels as if it's breaking me. Taste gunpowder on the places my skin is cracking from the heat. Falling in and out of war, I watch Seraphim come down to take the bodies of pirates to heaven.

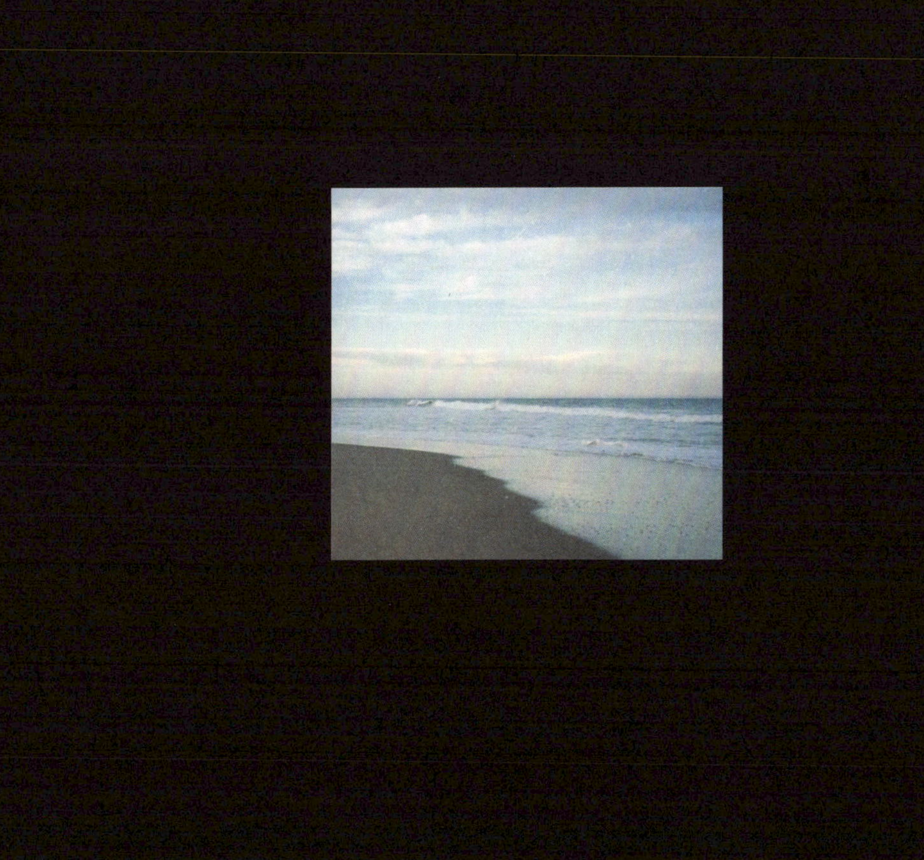

And the bards sang of him: Sheathed sword thrown into the hands of the sea. I draw in the tendrils that bind the beasts of the molten earth. Ride with them, demons. Ride with them.

Back in the old days (before Shenri, the two-headed jackal god of all people who wander, broke the skull of Craton to create the six seasons), Sio'kye, who the poets and bards call the right hand of the king slayer, was born to this earth. The son of a black dragon who fell for the pirate queen Yym-Kiy, who had given up her divinity as the goddess of wrath and those who cry in vengeance (she, who was the daughter of the beloved warrior goddess of farms and the food that keep the people fed, one of the elder original gods who farmers go to for safety in war: Mo). But his egg, born from the womb of his dragon father, did not stay safe for it was taken and corrupted by dark practices, by the Children of Light.

In their despair, his parents tried to find his egg to no avail. Sio'kye fought the demons of the depths that came to corrupt his body. Abandoning living in servitude under the church of light who had corrupted his soul, he was given a new form to hide within by the elder gods, who watched his noble spirit trapped within his draconian frame. Long black hair, eyes that glinted burning emerald. He joined the White Fire pirate crews that were under the god Soo Yeil's protection as they battled dragon egg hunters and were handsomely rewarded by the dragons of the known lands.

The bards sing of Sio'kye's nobility, though born a monster defying the nature of despair. They sing of when his pirate crew was taken by the Children of Light to their king, the blue-eyed lord of ice and hearth, Mykahlas. He who his children called "tormentor," who was born a peasant, and rose up to kill the old king of the northern lands who had sold his soul long ago for power. He who was in communion with the forbidden who live deep in the netherworld, gnashing their teeth.

They sing of the crew being taken before Mykahlas and when all hope was lost, Sio'kye breaking his human mirage to unveil, in horror and glory, his inhuman form to escape his shackles. They sing of him freeing his comrades and the battle that ensued. Of Sio'kye rising up and to protect his lover Mertagh, purple-eyed harpy elf of the desert lands. Of taking an arrow through his heart, giving Mertagh time to behead Mykahlas with the scimitar that was later named in ancient tongue, Ak'qiri (the quarter moon of Hiin'ui) to honor the two male lovers, for in ancient tongue Hiin'ui was the god of homoerotic rendezvous.

Sio'kye perished in the northern lands but his body was given to dragonkind and his claws were given to Mertagh, which he hung with gold rings from his wings. They say when you hear the pirate ships coming, they are like wind chimes in heaven's temples.

A lovers' song reflecting the rays of the sun.

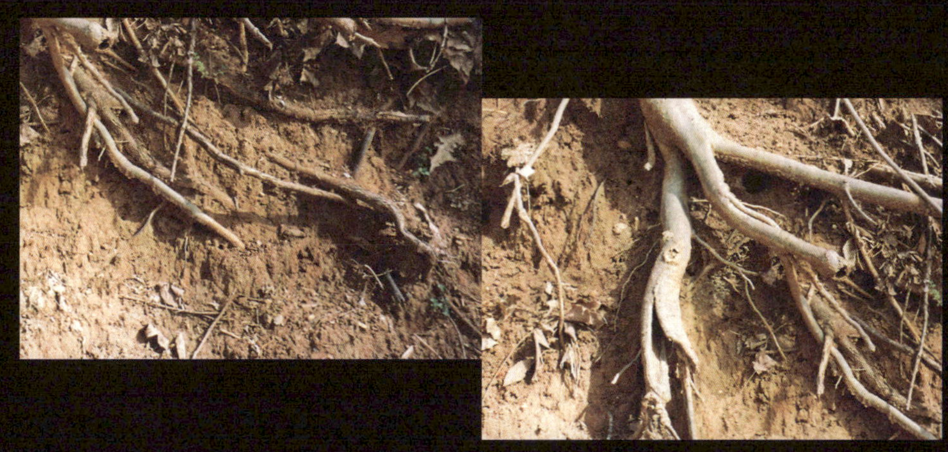

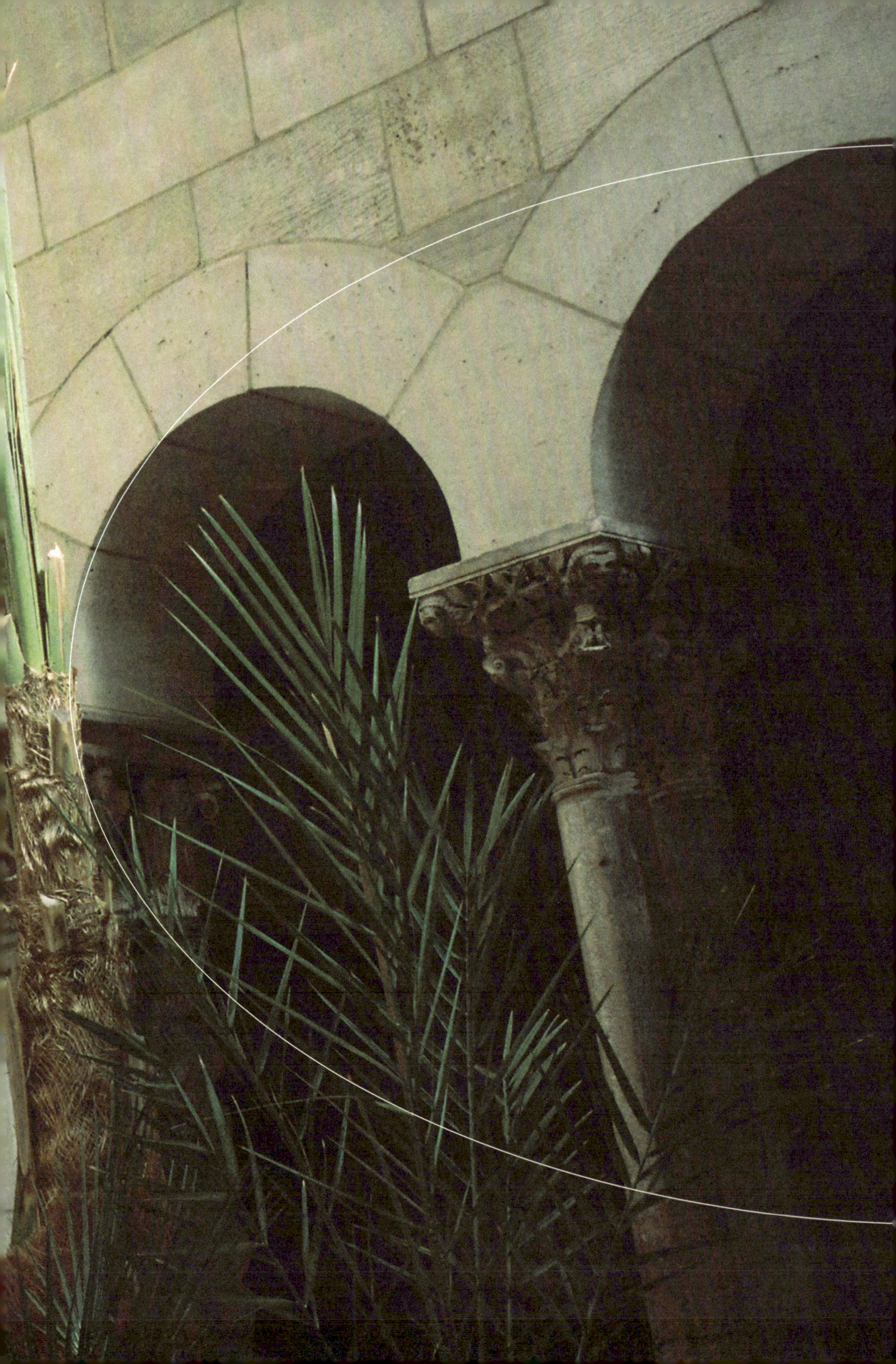

I DRINK
A GOBLET
OF OIL
AND
YOUR SPIT
CREATES
POOLS
WITHIN IT

PSALM OF WHITE FIRE

)00(DEMONIA

My blood is cunning.
Clever like a heathen king.
Knows when to lie.
I have always known when to lie
but never how long to keep it.
She gave this to me
wrapped in illness.

White rice. Soy sauce.
Butter. Garlic. I won't carry you out
of the car, but one day you're gonna
carry me down the stairs.

I drink a goblet of oil and your
spit creates pools within it
A mother licks the blood
off her newborn

Hair gets shorter with age.
Like blood, the lie touches sun spots
and gets kinder unlike its mother
Like age, hair gets thinner but like the
lie it stays jet black

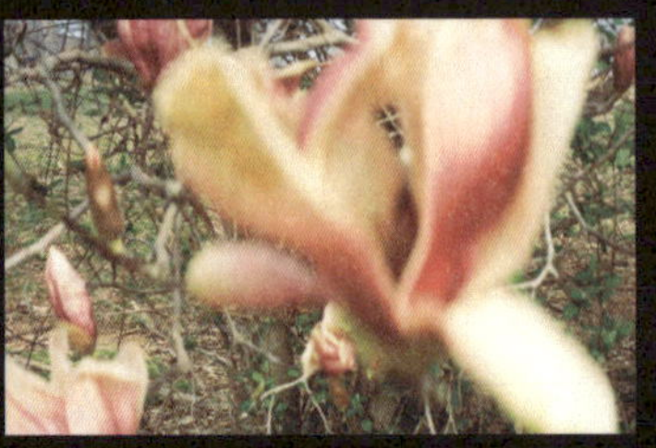

We all keep it jet black
Sister's sister dyeing hair
in the bathroom
I cover the scales on my cheeks
with foundation
I bite my claws off so they don't watch me
cut my skin open
on accident scratching myself because
I can't remember
how to count in the human tongues

Anger is the most fluid of all emotions.
What war machine, devotion,
chaos, it drives
Like a spirit, it comes inside of me,
pushing itself deeper into me
How it ravages the body leaving nothing
but dry ink and coins

Anger is cunning.
Coming only when thinking of blood,
age, hair. Comes when biting your nails.
I bite my nails when you lie.

)O(THE FAREWELL

Hoarse from the watcher
I swallow whole.
Oil and spit on my wings
we plummet –
Like the sound of ice crushing
under leather

Spiraling under twin stars,
in all of heaven's rotations,
there is an organ that plays for us.
Just as I am stripped from you,
malice is peeled to reveal
the sweetness of instead holding
an eternal myth.
As I am immortalized to you,
maybe it was better to lay my
sword
down in this way.

Losing you claims all of me.
When war ends you understand
the intimacy of silence,
two men's breath passing
through the other,
our heads are so close
I could press my forehead to you
but the mud cracks under you and
it is back to a battlefield
and the wind chimes
were metal breaking bone.

I leave this place to you
Gold in my back when they
take me to the pyre
You in my arms when judgment
is passed

This penance I carry and pay
for vengeance
A lie like a fine-tuned Sogongh
Rain baptizes me and honors me
Water understands distortion,
falsehood

Water understands sacrifice,
to be sacrificed

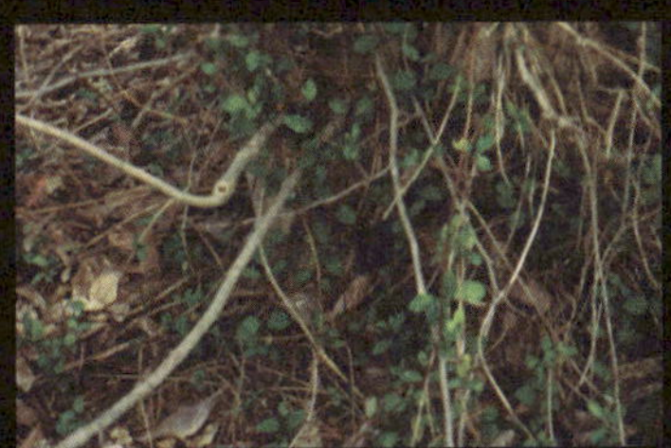

Pan

Pleasure hot like iron. They talked of the great god Pan, singing: as you hear his hooves, they ring out like the bells tied in the hair and ankles of the feral angels, heat in the body of those who run to the woods. When mortals heard his pipe, they were freed from their minds and filled with heat and madness, laying with beasts and breaking the chains of the kings who Pan refuted. They said that through Pan, the mountain pine spirit, and Sysiphos the nine harpy children were born. Sysiphos was a spirit that manifested as the giant white wolf, considered one of the old gods who had returned to the split earth. Pan the half goat lay with his lover, the white wolf, in a field of epiphyllum oxypetalum in full bloom. One hundred years later, their harpy children emerged from the ground, long after their fathers had left the split earth to return to Airos, the spherical planet where water and earth met, bringing with them their congregation and cult of madness.

The children:

With the faces of mortals, legs and arms (wings) of great birds of prey, these children were called the children of the sea sky that was created by the new world's first wild gods. In these days, you could look up and witness the sea. The world was like two flat trays facing itself with stars, the sun, the moon going between them like a tunnel. The sea above, the land below: so the mortals deemed the harpy children sirens, for they flew through mortal sky, but through what the harpies knew as sea.

PT.05

FORKED TONGUE

FREE DESIRE

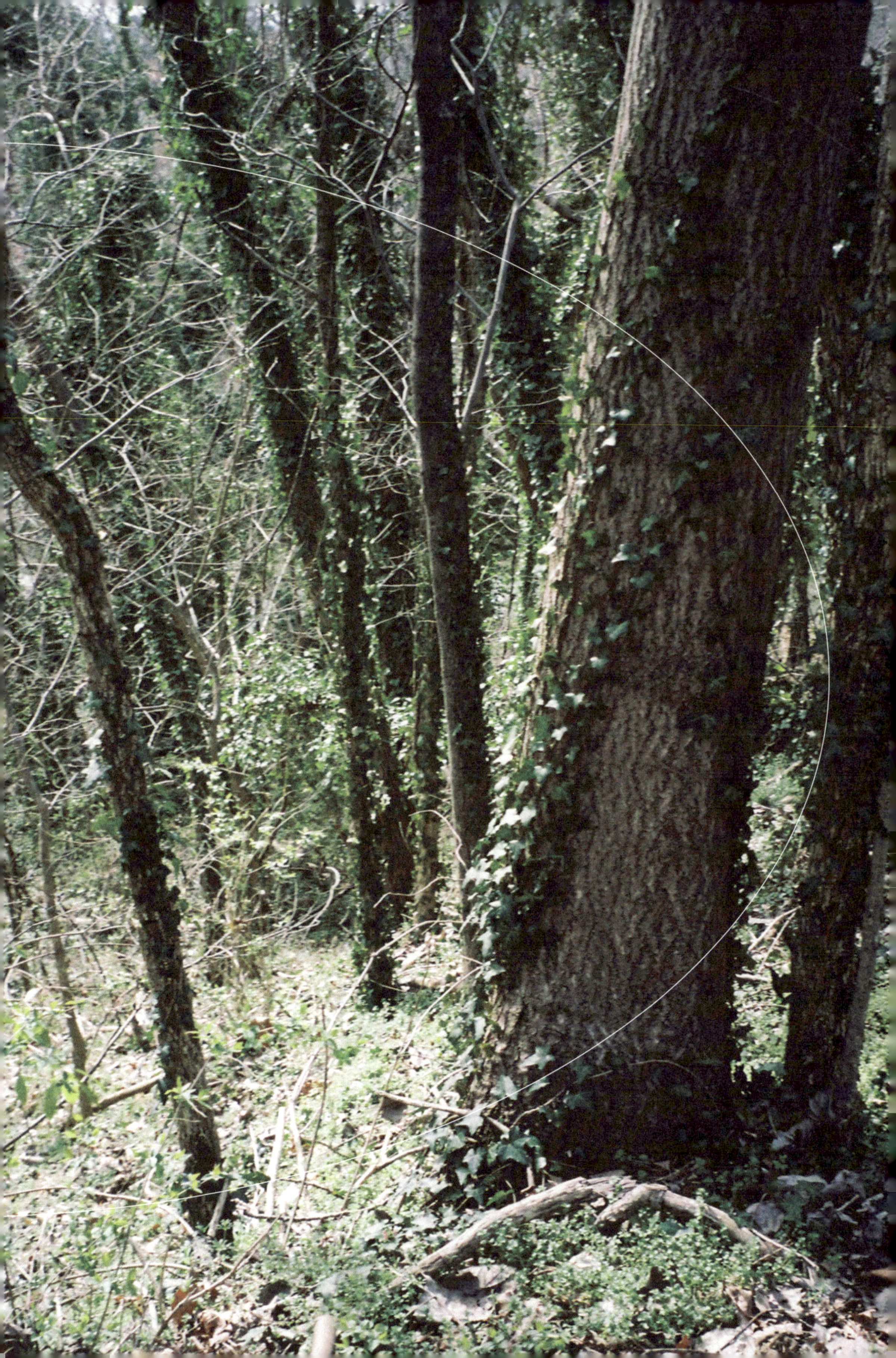

PSALM OF PAN

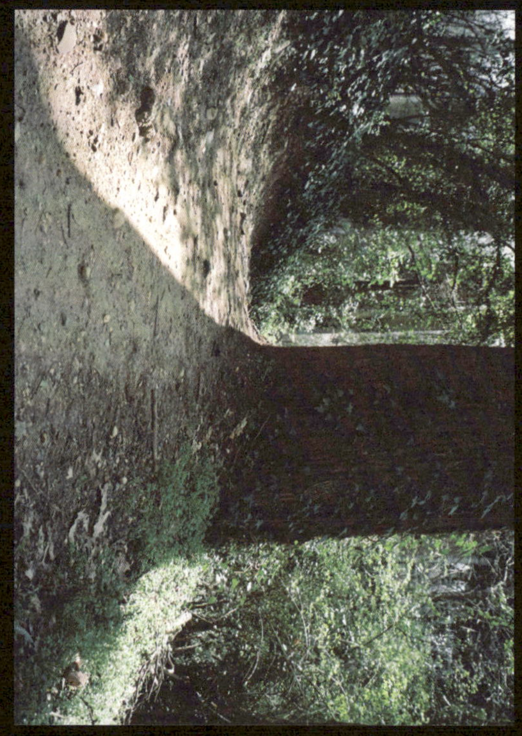

Humanity's war on desire stretches its arrogance and cowardice towards nature. The constant verge that the breath of men hinges on between yearning and fate. What are carnal calls on the pan pipes, in my hesitation I pull you towards me. In my acceptance we caress one another gently in the dark. And the vibrance of our hair as Gaia blesses us with tens of thousands of leagues we tie together.

Jealousy rests in her heart, the trees bare in fall, fear in her hands,
wavering voice.

Crying blood, red-eyed from smoke, singing and screaming at the moon you run from your lover, leave her, bed still warm, barefoot on wet mud and grass, the pipes beckon like silk slithering around the body.

Forked tongue, free desire.
The taste of salt far from the sea.

Your legs belong to the earth, just as the carnal gods made the stones and the vultures too made the capacity in the hearts of humans to crack. Splitting like pain drumming in the night, daughters break from the skulls of their fathers. Splitting like knowing no shame or regret.

Anointed with ecstasy
And with pleasure comes responsibility. discipline. freedom. choice.

Humanity's dependence on jealousy and shame is venom they spit into the mouth of their lover. Three canine teeth, two next to one another like solemn dancers. Tornado – but it's two dryads swaying together.

"you look as if you're always somewhere far away"

In the early days of the mortal structures (when they learned to find dominance over one another), the kings of earth paid hefty tribute to each of the four winds. But the tribute was not that of gold, but of prosperity in their kingdoms. The four winds valued mortal joy, for they understood the value of it as immortal beasts.

The vampire lords: Vi'jir (the cutting Northern breeze), Hero'th (the planetary prevailing Western wind), Vilae (the untouchable Eastern gale), and Raya (the empress of Southern trade winds). The four winds were known to be terrible and generous. Mighty in their eternal knowledge and wrathful in their infernal wisdoms. Each lived at their respective corners of the earth and would wander towards the great capital, a one hundred year journey one way, training great warriors, musicians, scholars, alchemists, and artists. When they met in the center of the world, at the time of the planetary alignment, the sun would turn black and night would overtake the earth. Many songs were sung until the sky would crack and the dragon that was seen as a pure body of pink flame would drag the sun and all of its children deep into the crypts, deep in the heart of space. The sky would be left with a ring of fire where the sun used to reside. Burning the infinite circle into the hearts of men.

And they rebuke war, famine, Hades, and conquest. What use are immortals that are contrived by the fears of those who may pass on? They drink the blood of wild horses and the sun shines a brilliant opalite hue, blinding those that look at their lips dripping with the crimson petals of life.

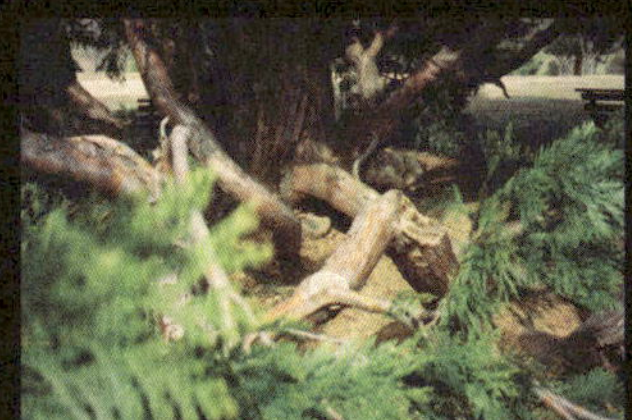

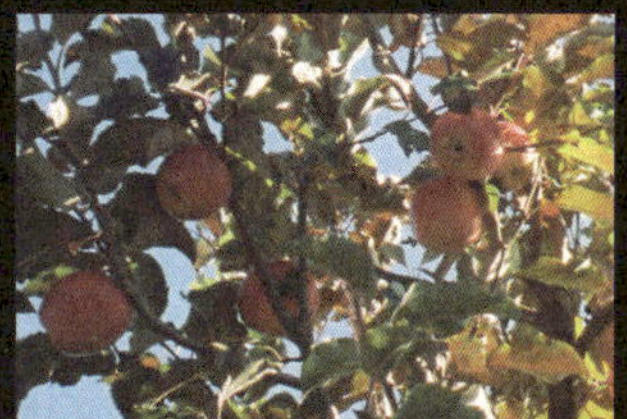

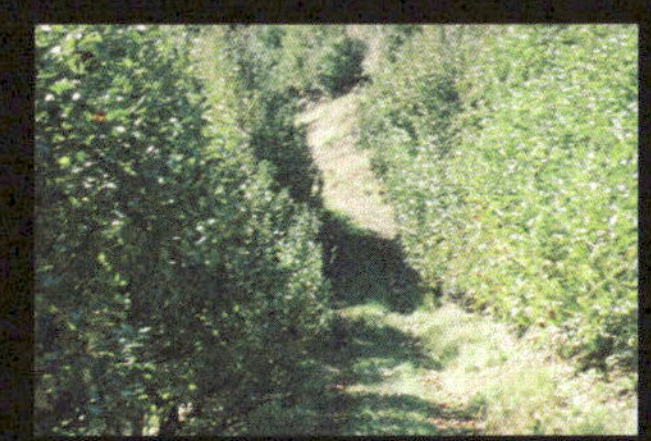

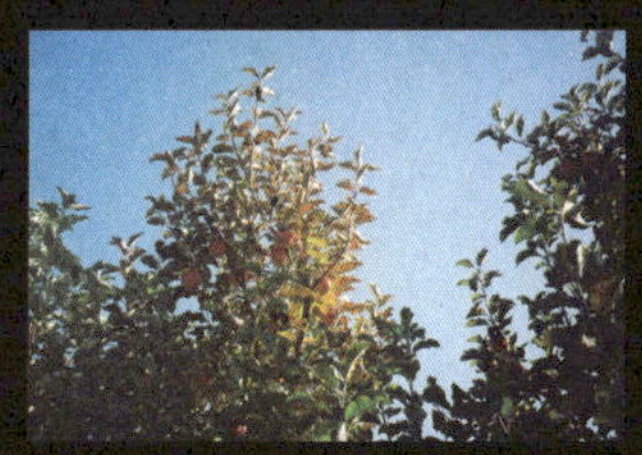

Mochihira

Mochihira. Holiest of all women. The holiest of all mothers. Who cradled her child in her two arms and with the other two held the bow and arrow of Ziphaa. She who was born before the wolf god Anu was still whole. Mochihira was a mortal woman. Desired by some god of little consequence. He chased her to a temple of one of the mortal gods and when he tried to assault her, she cried out.

The goddess of that temple did not answer.

But the elder deity Keida heard Mochihira's cries. Xe (Keida) froze time and came to her and asked for her greatest desire. Mochihira answered power and Keida in approval gave her a body and heart of power – half her body that of a great serpent, four arms, and long emerald hair as black as the sea and green as the sea in the sunlight. And when time reemerged xe was gone, but Mochihira reared up against the lesser god and killed him, tearing out his heart and liver.

> Ziphaa, one of the harpy children of Pan and Sysiphos, who was watching from the mirror that all memory flows, then reached through time and space to give their bow to Mochihira, charging her with immortality. They blessed the arrows to only harm those with impure intention.

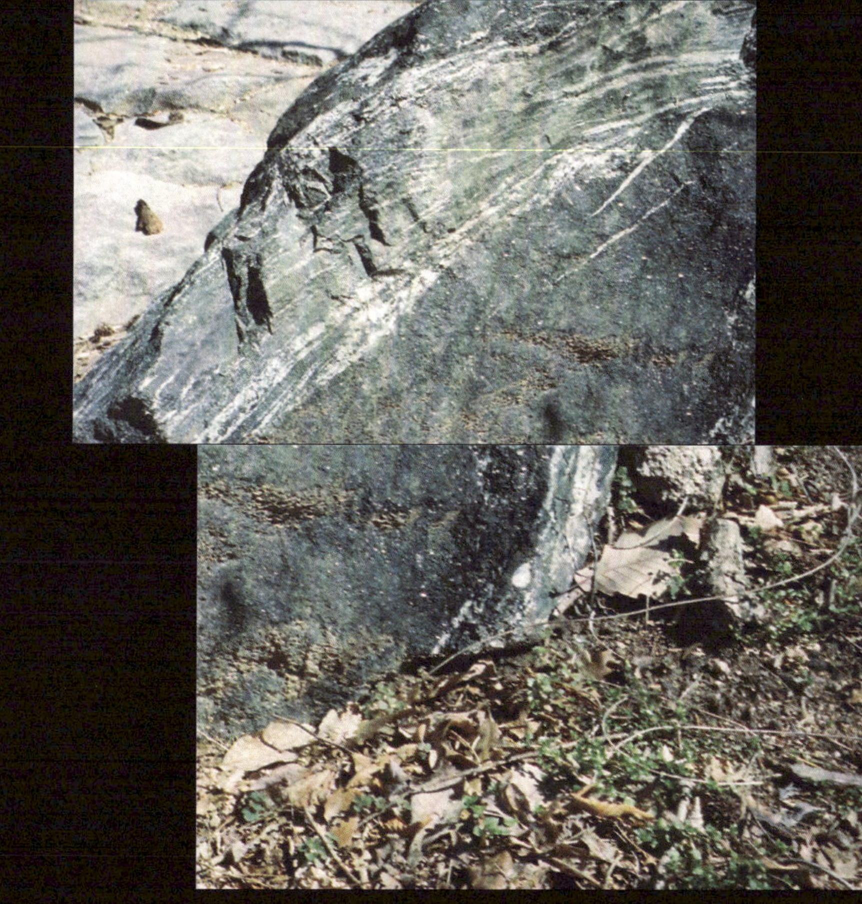

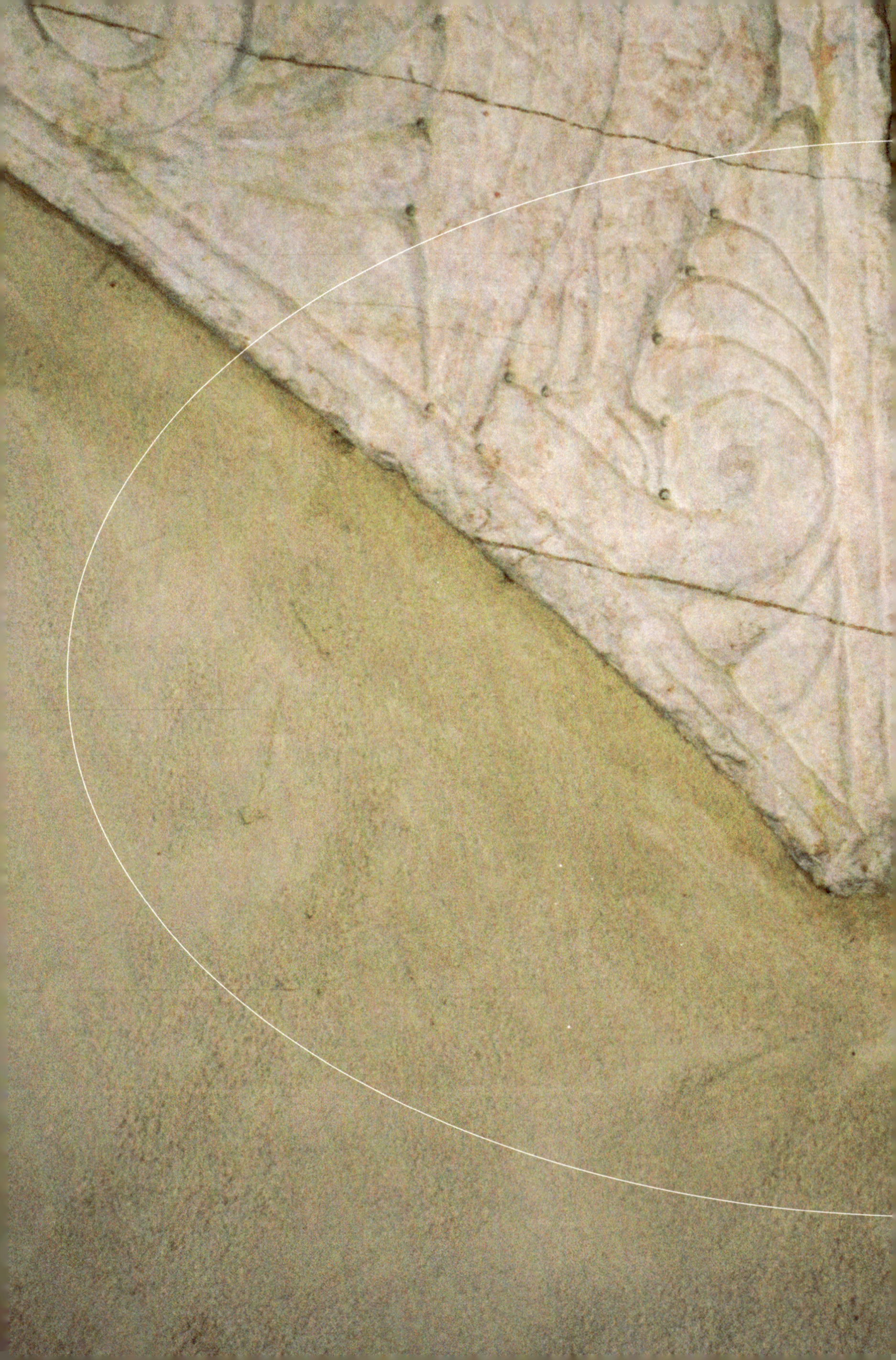

MEMORY TURNS TO DUST IN THE WAKE OF POWER

We will not wait for the
ancestors to hear our prayers
For what gods they paid allegiance to
will open the gates?

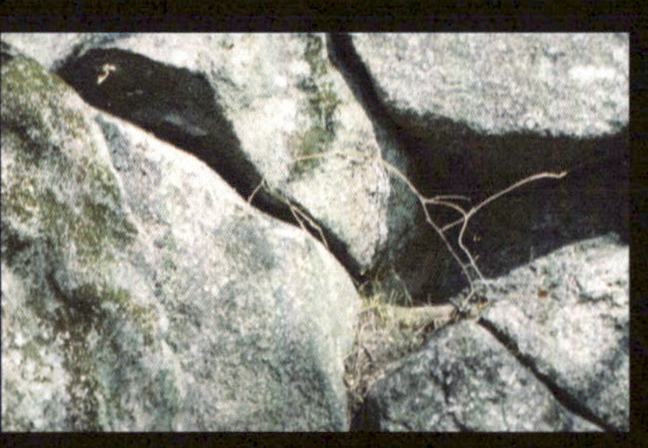

Mortals will burn angels at the stake
and call it the will of god.

Carve out on the maps of
your body where you have
resisted death

In her arms you press into
the concrete

When the car crashes
wraiths take your
liver from your corpse

You're dead, but you're beautiful.

Moonshine that he used
to make in his bathtub
burns holes in the bedsheets

You move away but
he chews incense –
tobacco and bourbon,
pine needles, and fat
You taste it on his fingers,
because of him you taste it
on your dreams

Like tar bubbles we rip open,
porous in the desert
Melt that shit in the heat
In dreams you find no solace

your dreams are in the hands
of the gods now
And what serves you has
never been from the heavens

In the pit you find
your kind of people.

You return to what you know.
Who will teach you honor?
Who will teach
you to feel strong?

Your mother
whose mind is lost?

Your father who
wept in insincerity?

Coal from the fire
soaks in their weakness.
You didn't cry when
lesser gods pulled you
under the water.

When lesser gods
of plague violated you.

The response in vulnerability
should have been your right.

You learn to hold your tears because
they are the currency of revenge

Your vengeance
won't be cheap like that
It will be that which goes
in the palms of
heartless bastards
If you crawl on your belly
you can never be their dog

Surname erased from the
annals of history.

You want to be adorned in
beauty but it ever eludes you
Punished for nothing, you:
deformed by the judgment of law

In secret spaces your sweat
is the covenant of arrogance
In secret spaces you
serve yourself
Lean into it
Brutality is a lover
of the two-faced
Lead liars in a rebellion
against purity

And when you smell liquor
on their breath you start spinning
All of it –
And his memory is turned to
dust in the wake of power
An arrow passes through
the bathroom window,
Now you don't take the
emergency exit, you stand
white-knuckled
Lead pipe called Excalibur

Your heart races
It's exciting to hurt bad men.

Death God

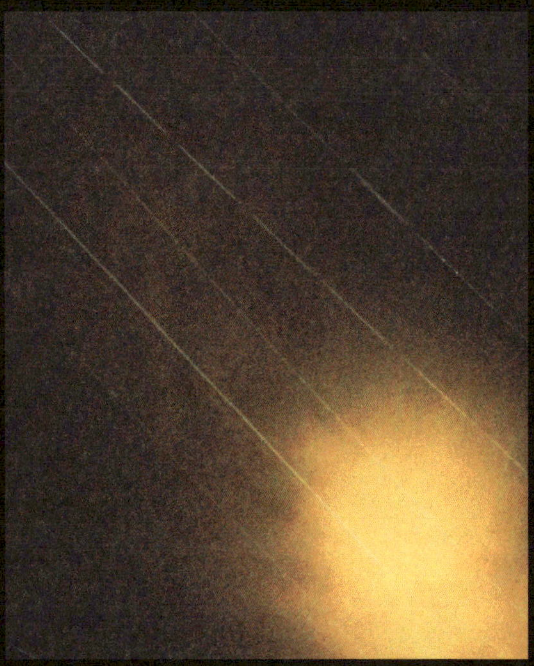

In the deserts of Sakiiro

Setith (scimitar of the southern lands), the Cobra Wyvern in the desert (called by the people of these lands), was said to be the father of burying the dead. For he, a deity by any right, held court in the pearl of the oasis: Yilig-ata, the tomb of a thousand rooms. It was said that it was constructed of pure pearl and white marble. In each room were beautiful statues of all the fallen heroes. Their recorded memory was on silk as thin as moth wings, fluttering from the glass-domed ceilings. The guardians of the Wyvern's palace were said to be a race of mixed orc/elf. Beautiful and aged as the desert mountains. Like a sandstorm that destroys the earth, yet libra lilies grow ten times stronger. The palace was a space of refuge for the bodies of the fallen, left on the altars of jade until the mortal vessel would rot and decompose to dust. The dust was then taken and placed in the eternal flame and their soul would be welcome to stay in the palace for as long as they wished. It was a holy space.

A space of pleasure beyond the human imagination. In a place where the night is a lavender haze where no shadow falls. But in reckless elegance, the spirit of Seokga lost its way when the dust of their frame did not completely enter holy fire, setting the hundred year pilgrimage of Setith to fly to far lands to retrieve the wanderer.

And when Seokga's spirit was found, it fell madly in love with the Death God, who returned their passions in such fever the pantheon turned in disgust, for what frivolous feelings does a Death God throw to the spirits of mortals? Yet Seokga's spirit could not stay on earth, for though they were the half-son of Loki, god of mischief, they never completed their great odyssey which all demis are cast upon – and thus never reached immortality.

The gods of the deep catalyzed heaven to demand Seokga's spirit be released into the courts of Yilig-ata. But the dust of Seokga's body had gone far in the desert and not all could be found, though Setith searched for eight thousand years. Their lover's soul was barred from the heavens. The infernal vampire kings (the four winds) were charged to hold court and their verdict was for Setith to never allow a situation where another soul would be barred from eternity. The great god of death then forbade the burning of the bodies of earth and instead formed the endless Catacombs of Azule beneath the second underworld for bodies to decay. Souls would no longer stay on earth and take a time of pleasure or rest before the next life, but instead pass straight through the cosmos.

The only soul to remain on this earth now is that of Seokga, half-son of Loki. His spirit can be seen resting on the shoulder of the Death God in his empty halls as the three-headed jackals bury the dead of the world and spread gospel to all nations to do the same. Over the eons, Setith released mankind of this charge and humans took control of their own dead and the souls of mortals were given back to themselves to do with after death as they saw fit, creating the era of the ever-gods – the reign of the post-human where life was precious and none feared death.

DEATH
IN ITS
VARIANT
FORMS
APPEARS AS
OBSTACLES
OF PINING.

WHY COULD I NOT BE SLAIN BY MAN?

PSALM OF SETITH

For what is lost, my love, in fleeting snow?
As ice I see like a first sunrise tears and gnaws at the fabric
of our embrace

Flee from me as I drive you from fate's volley
As your spirit rises into the bows of the willow
Heat and desolation are embroidered through my cloak
As I keep the souls of the living in my wake
Bountiful is the harvest, softer beyond measure is the fruit
Skin bursts as you pluck it from the tree

The desert plays tricks and I tell you once again I find
solace in the mirage
The whole time as I look through you and find love
this is the same tenderness that comes to me
as I look through the water
no man may drink.

Sand in the bloodstream of heathens,
Hold up the ashes and lips in the wind kiss you
I pull you close to me like mist in the gardens

We call hell Eden, for what do mortals know
of the divide between worlds?

You raise the winds within me.
I am left gasping and in that space a force no fury may restrain,
you call it sentiment – it sinks, or disperses the swell of your
confinement to air, it releases me.

To lose your fetter we are lost to one another,
To loosen that celestial tempest that pleasure cannot subdue
I am bound to you. And loss bears my train, loss caresses me

A loss we call duty which I am bound to fulfill
gnashes at your fairness,
quivering in the hollow wound you leave in me.
You dance aloft in the air from the touch of gods.
Cables crack. Foam at the corners of my lips.
The confusion of the roar between death and longing for spirits,

The gods may die of thirst just as they may die of desire,
a force far more violent than thirst.

A transient ravishing.
Your faces renew me
I want you
Death in its variant forms appears as obstacles of pining.
Why could I not be slain by man?
Noble lover, our fates bewail us.

Descend into me, your spirits passing me
When morning rose into view I show tombs
spacious above the floods.
The trembling in the deep is lost and you come out of me.
No less faithful than when you entered.

No goodbyes to those not truly lost. This is the lament of I, who admit the deluge of such a steady stream of love that I cast aside to fulfill all fates that govern. For what love does not fear the reign of destiny's envy? We are not lost to one another. This is our shadowed glance cast to that which governs god.

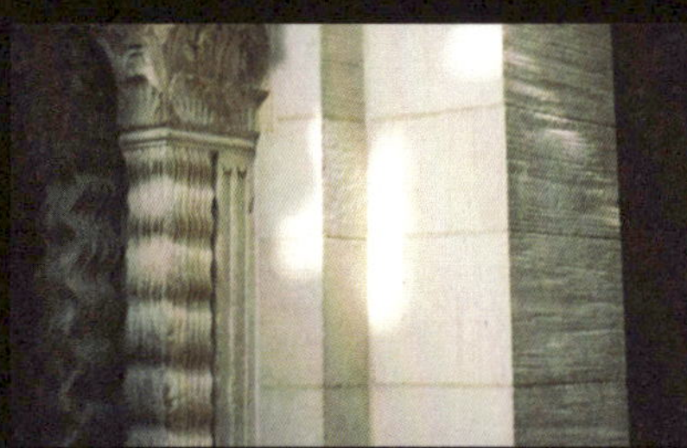

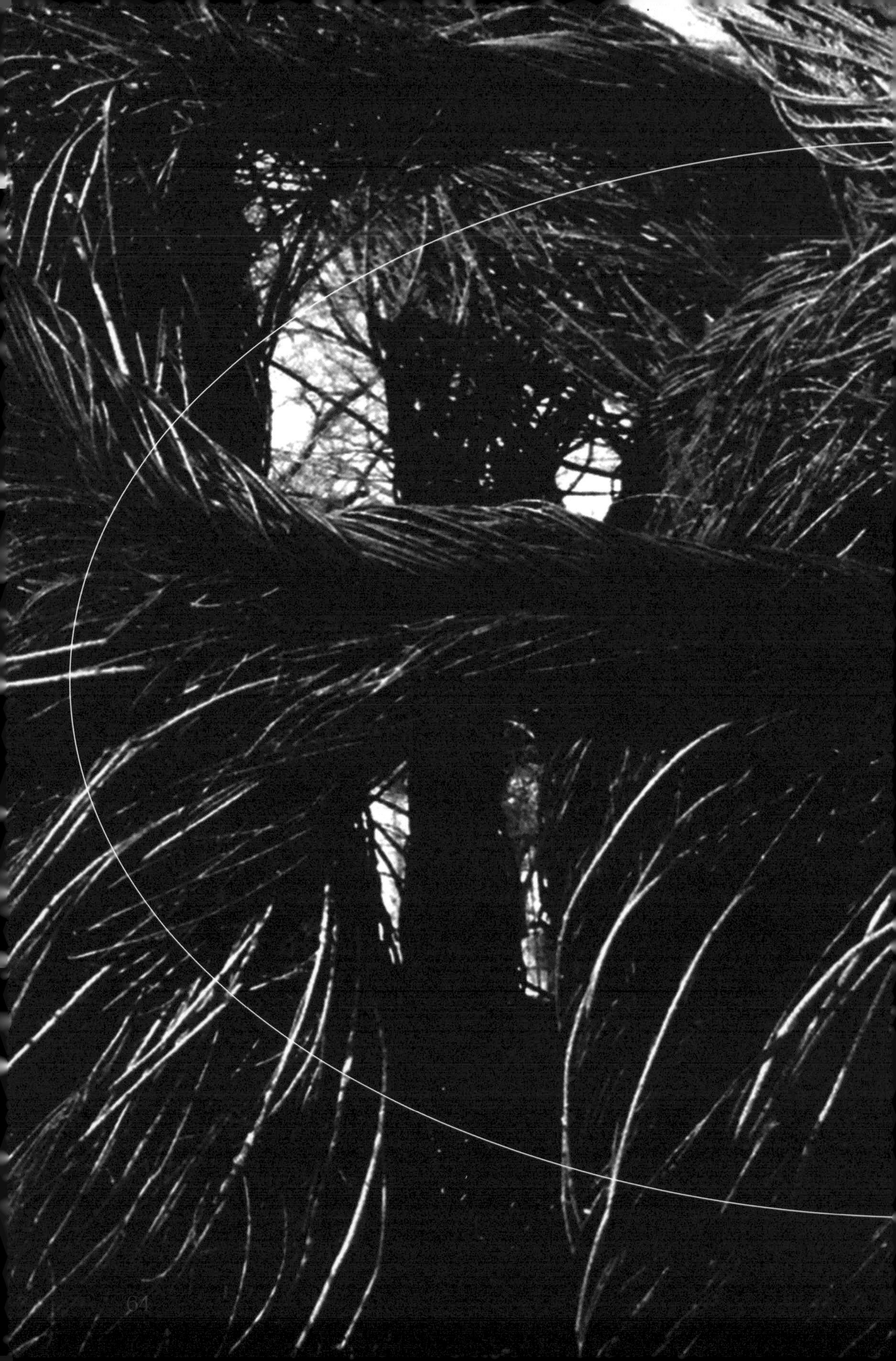

OLD TESTAMENT

TOIL

My feelings fleeting, beautiful and terrible as the storm
and the places the tender of this world hide
Where does the moth seek shelter from Ragnarok?
When they emerged, restored as a blue dawn
Fell as the mad tongue reigning in the deep

Spit drips from my lips to the mouth of woe
Boys pulled to their death
Of what kelpie do the hymns sing?
Here stood the rumors seated on the ancient sea
The break between bathed in the mightiness of myth,
Instead I am scattered with the remnants of discontent.
The lengths the devil's labor treads for such a fame

A scarce toil for the glory of being truly seen
To be truly seen by you
The mortals fear that which can "kill" them.
But where is their understanding of fear?
Do they not birth it from the depths
of their long unhappy storms?

I ask them again, let's not exist.
But we are so seen.
We are so terrifyingly visible to them.
We press for release, the impatient captive,
to feel truly alone
and unwatched.

Why the water and a feminine vengeance?
The siren wraps their arms around me as a Piscean deity.
And will the secret seeds of envy for those who feel assured in their natural identity lay waste to a heart already full of reflective disdain?

The whirlwind of the deep.
They talk of injustice.
Of "unfair."
Of innocence.
A sounding tempest that is a fruitless force
For what voice do humans have?
Pity. Greed. Joy. Survival. Adoration.
The wretch hisses in flames

They worship god and they worship themselves
and they worship one another,
As a trembling game with fury, fraught with devastation.

That which I hurl against the mountain side,
a wave so great it engulfs the universe.
The first storm of the world.

They named the naiad Ilromyn, the bearer of the first storm.
For their grieving was great for the friend they had lost to
the greed of the wars of men.

THE CHAIN

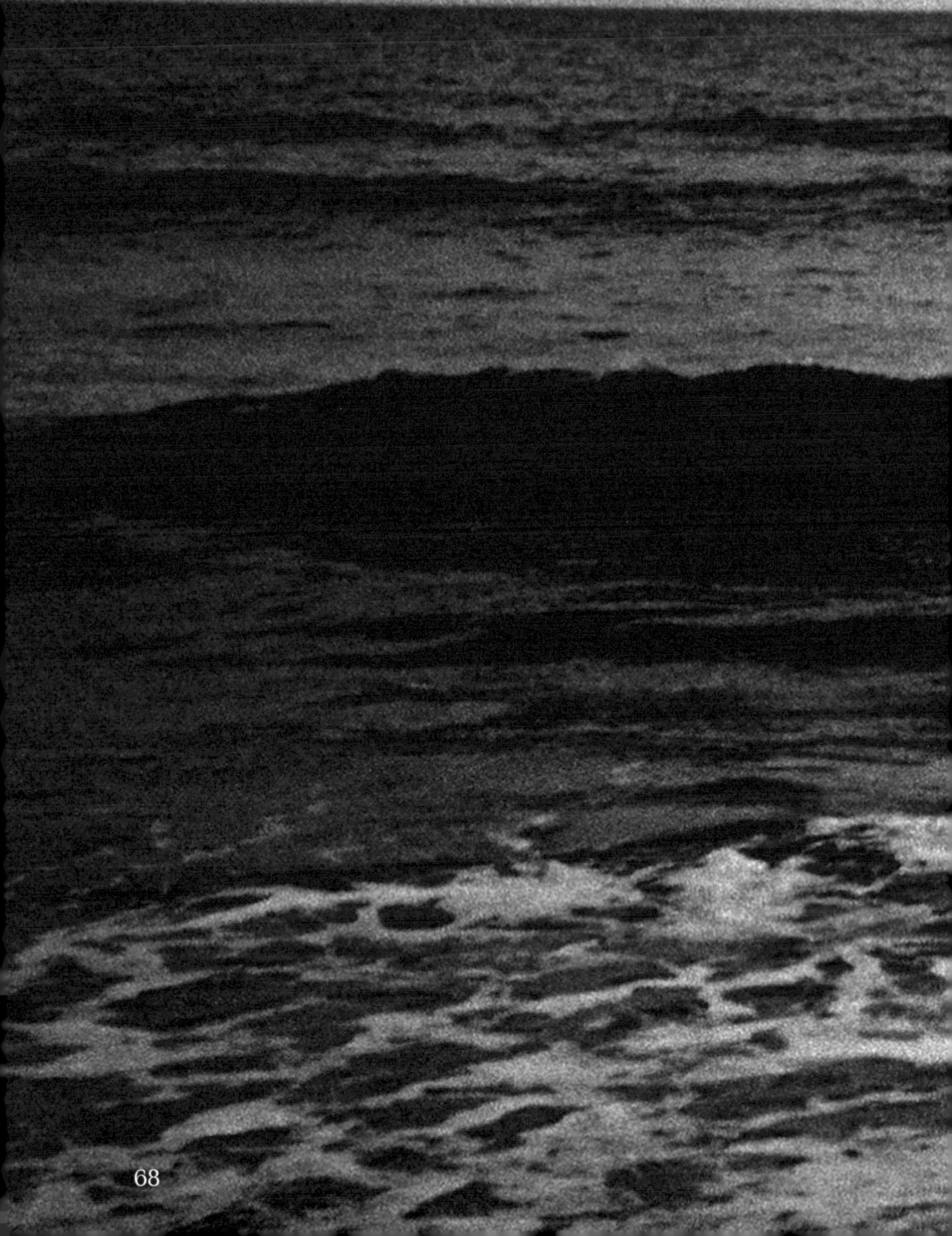

To the companions of cruel desire – sacrificed on the altar of the sea. There was Ithoryn, the one who was mist over saltwater, the one who sang sailors to their death. Then seeing her rows of fangs ungodly, they would be seized with mortal fright as their flesh made feast for beauty.

Sorrow streamed from the eyes of the drow, Sydral, who captained the ship shattered upon stone. Watching as her crew became banquet for fell creatures. She was taken by Ithoryn, who fell in love with the captain, to the deep caves below the water and held captive there. She was scorned by her kind and the two wandered the many islands of Iros'tirin. Sydral took her back to her lands but they shackled Ithoryn to great stones and left her to die at the seafloor. Sydral despaired at being unable to save her lover from eternal bondage and would dive as far as she could, but was always unable to reach her.

The goddess Letru took pity on the lovers, but the lands where Ithoryn was bound were governed by a spiteful god, Ekvir, fattened on human sacrifice. Letru asked the lovers their wish and it was simply to be together in any form, but she could not act as long as Ekvir reigned over those lands. She struck him down with holy thunder and bound him under the water and Sydral and Ithoryn clasped hands and lips and became the sacred chain that binds Ekvir in his crypt. The chain sings a deadly hymn that keeps the spirit of the fell god in his slumber as the two stay in eternal embrace, protecting the lands of men from the fell god. Vows offered as solemn prayer made borrowed shapes of love to bind eternal and ensnare the demon god Ekvir. Consummated in molten iron and anointed in heaven's eyes.

THE SPINE

The tiefling Aranthus slept with the ox god Sokro at the festival of stars in the day, where the feral deities wandered the lands of mortals. Cian-Li, the first minotaur, was born from his father's back and was the twelfth of the children of heaven to spawn in the fields of men. Aranthus and Sokro made a deal with Bacchus to send their son to protect the village from the death spirit, Malu'kuart (the two-headed serpent of Hades).

With the bones of the hydra, the fell weapon Vishgale (the first longbow) was made. It was placed in the hands of Cian-Li, who took a sacred oath to Bacchus to serve him as all the twelve children of earth did, under the four moons of Nom-Ara. Cian-Li shot a single arrow through the four eyes of Malu'kuart and completed seven feats for seven years in the service of his patron. Bacchus then took Vishgale and hung it in the hall of kings. Two eras later, he lay with a mortal man Hi'rrah and from his womb the satyr, Vega, was born, who wielded Vishgale in the later wild hunts of the higher gods who turned against the deities of the wood.

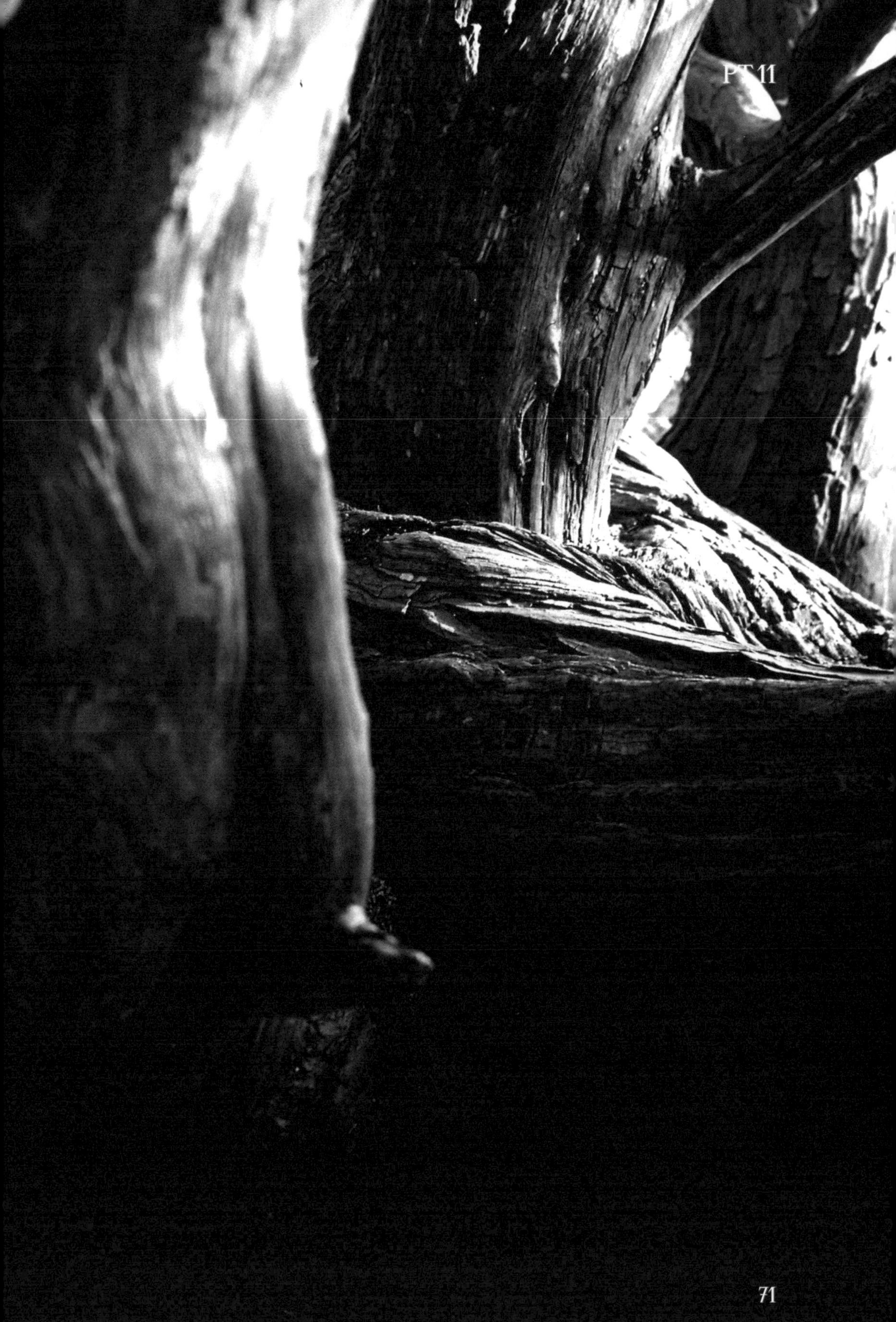

PT 11

THE BELLS

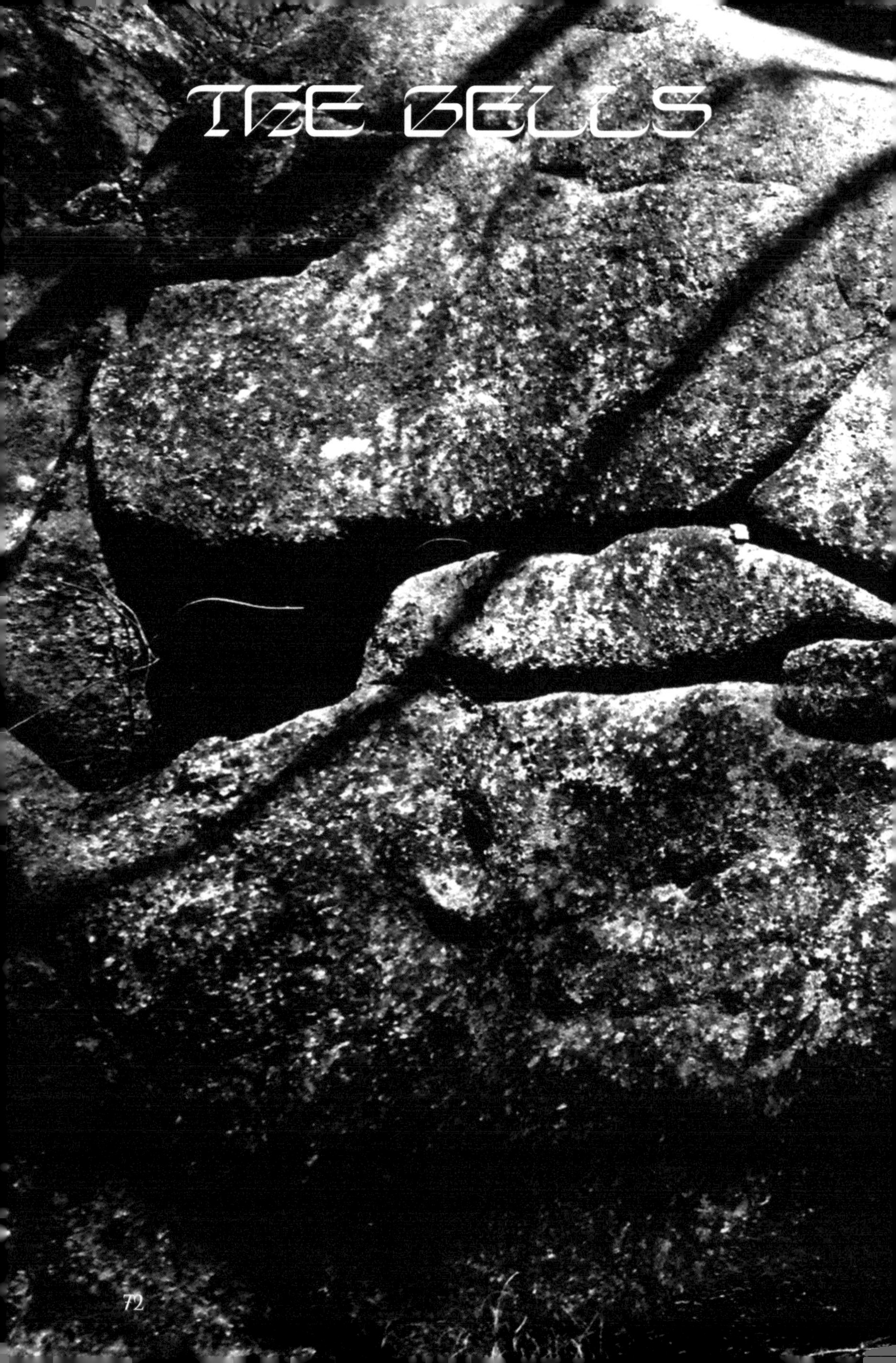

The prince of thieves, Cala (a kenku) ran the House of Oracle, the sanctuary of all species established secretly in the catacombs under the pearl city of Golhildil. The kenku were banned from the skies after the uprising of Ellu. The great songs told of Cala saving the House of Oracle by performing the miracle of the bells, summoning a storm so great that all on the surface were swept away by the winds before ever reaching the underground. He did this by cutting out his own heart and offering it to Illinan, the spirit of disaster.

Blessed in sights unknown,
Those with no heir and no need calling upon
the sky to pour forth –
Wither did you fly Cala? One who made
the shoulders of the great reach the ground.
Before reaching that passage unseen,
performed solemn prayer and bleeding heart,
When the enemy nearer in distance,
making their ascent, found themselves swept up
in the encore of the great martyr.
Now ordained the prince of thieves.

THRESHOLD

In the time after the great fire, which divided humans and the other races of the two earths due to the grave holy war, Sezshei, a yuan ti, was caught during a raid on the lands of Ur'zere'nd and brought to the human city of Ma'lag'an. Before their execution, a khezrethih follower of the old gods took mercy on Sezshei and gave them a temporary shapeshifting spell to escape the axe in time to find refuge in the city's temple of Soo Val.

Soo Val was praised as the god of those between forms and emotional changelings, whose temple still remains a sanctuary to all, for none may commit violence when crossing the threshold. If violence is done, Soo Val (in all of his glory) appears and instantly turns them to sand. Protector of all in his temple from violence, born out of the side of Soo Yeil.

The elemental gods were seen as the only "true teachers" and thus feral gods like Soo Val were said to have left this dimension for another in the great pilgrimage. The feral gods still accepted blood sacrifices and would still walk among all mortal creatures. The elemental gods were considered the champions of "humanity" (human kind). Their forefathers, the Counsel of Ariachille, had formed humans from clay, fire, salt, and the tongue of the brightest of stars, and gave them willingly to make the new species. Humans were not the only species created, but, in their selfishness, claimed the elemental gods.

A hundred altars in a temple of smoke.

But Sezshei, now cursed to remain in the temple empty of heaven's presence for fear of execution, fell deeply in love with the form of Soo Val, and in his desperation to see the god but with no earthly belonging, cut off his right hand and offered it up on the altar. And Soo Val, who had made the pilgrimage as some said, smelled hot iron and felt the call of the old world and chose to return and appear in his glory in front of Sezshei. He restored his hand and hearts soared and the two men became lovers, told in the songs that have vanished from modern temples. For Soo Val chose to honor Sezshei and his sacrifice by granting him the immortal flame that burns in the hearts of the gods. They rest in the fields of Bellehim where the water is sweet and an eternal spring blooms.

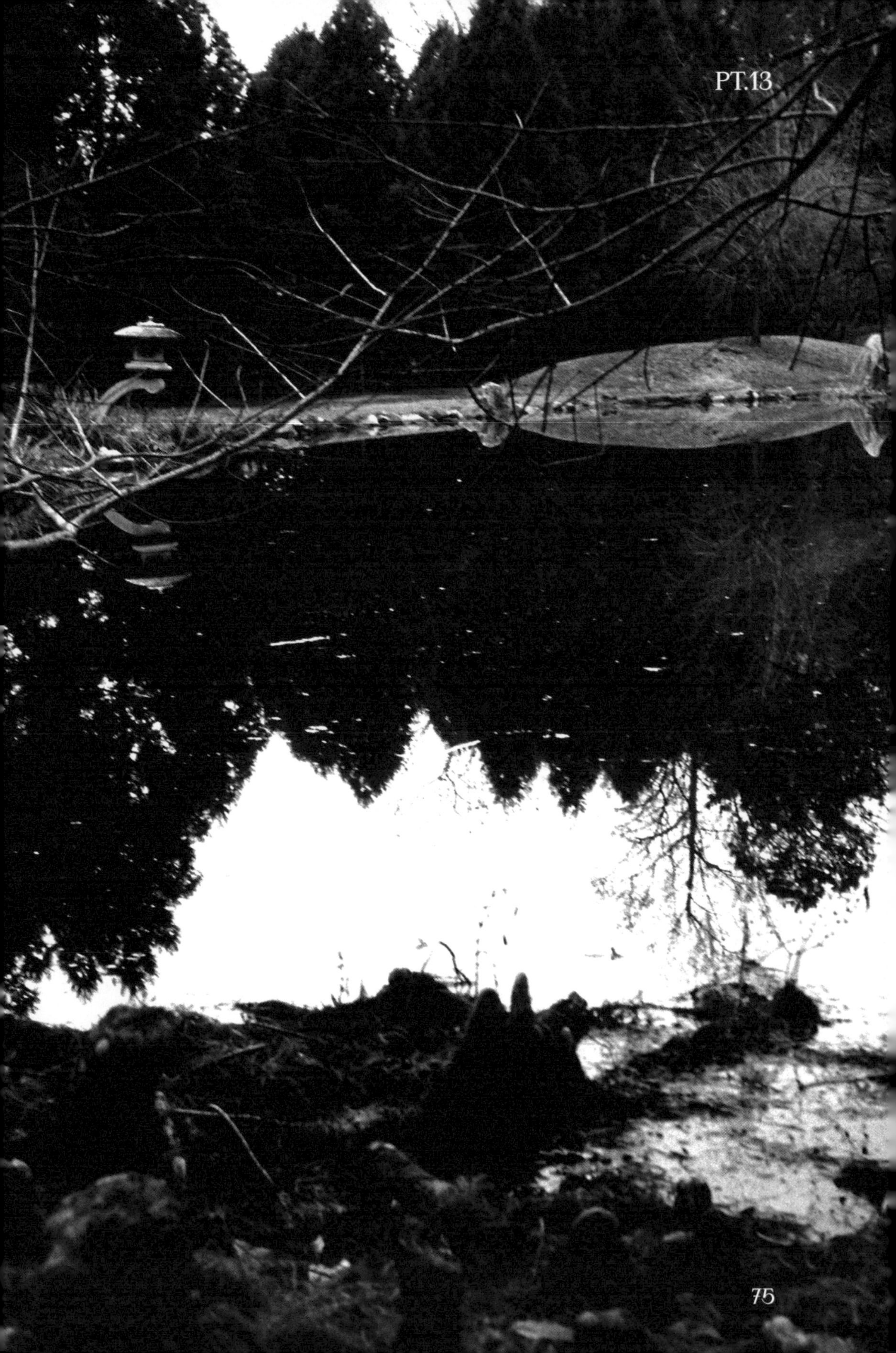

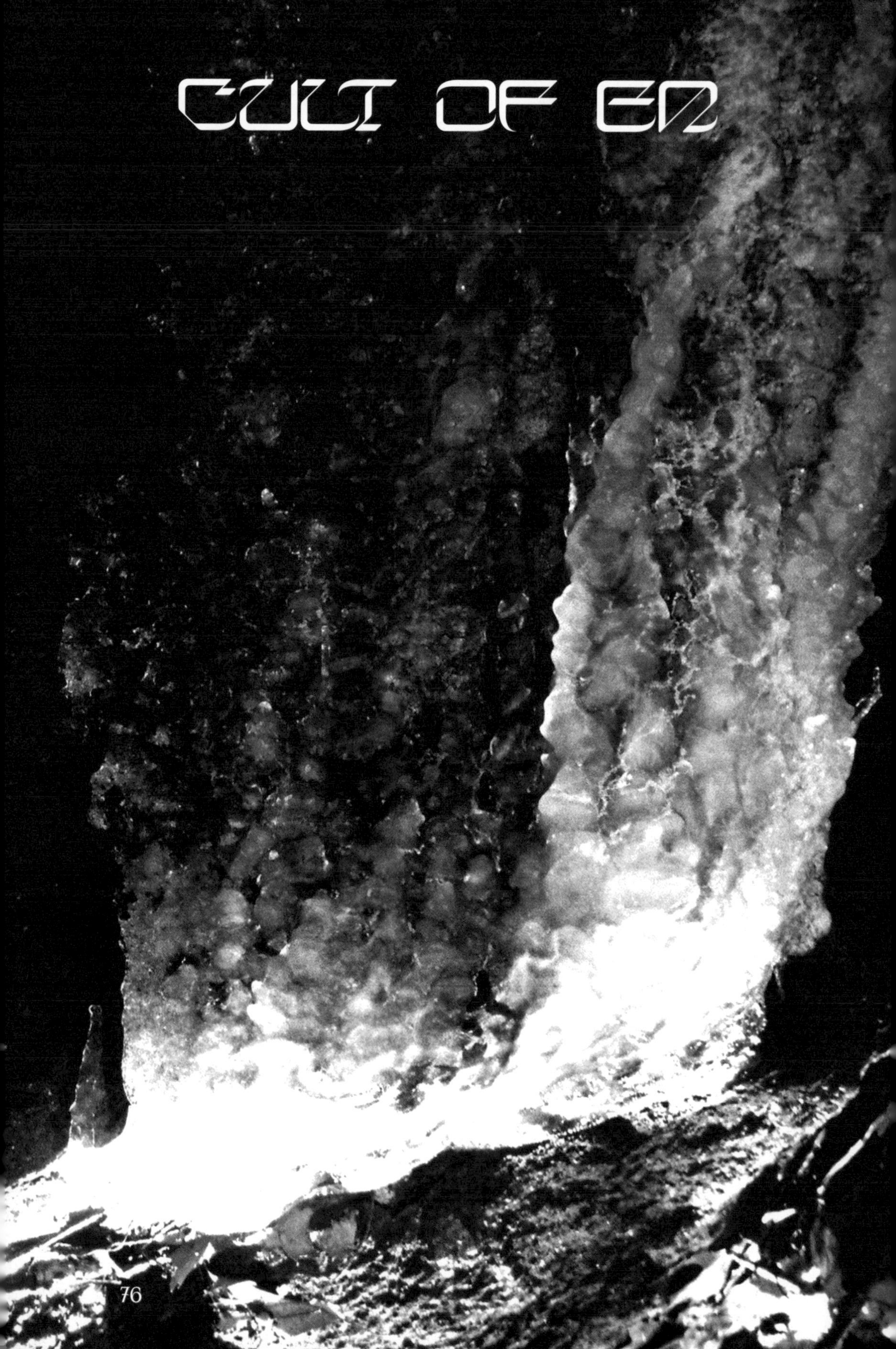
CULT OF EM

Of what goddess did we provoke to offend heaven like this? To which the stars rest in the belly of great fish. The scales which cut our hands, you hold tighter as its body thrashes against you. Such resentment shows from the depths, I was there at the dawn of such sentiments. I beheld the unmitigated call of ningyo, who cut the great fish and served the stars marinated in its stomach acids. The Cult of Ea, the first in line for the feast of the heavens.

In the order of the regale:

RIGEL
VEGA
ALTAIR
ARCTURUS
ALGOL
ALNILAM
SAIPH

Hunger flies before the driven soul, I want you in my belly more than I want you in my guts. The vore of the universe, swallowing a solar eclipse wet green light dizzying.

Taking one by one in, the seasonal festivus of the glutton and summer haze. The labor of the sun to protect its brethren as it was pulled down by ropes to set. The golden burden taken and stored for the haze of what is to come. Mortals who feasted on starlight. Coerced in some headstrong envy, they were driven by some unknown force of will against the night sky.

GUNPOWDER

With monotonous regularity blood is washed from the clothes and we hang them as striga in the fields. A woman with a gun, a dangerous adversary of kings.

> The strength of this attachment
> Of no desire of the good opinion of the gods
>
> The acknowledgement of their regard
>
> Stronger than the foundations of the earth
>
> We talk of gambling with the fates
> I have found a way to hedge my bets
>
> As their rage commands
>
> Unresisted sway

Was first made from grinding the bones of chaos to dust. A powder the solemn smoked and the brazen and fierce placed in fire.

The wars of fame which courage expelled, brave were the men who met the sword with eyes alive with the songs of their forefathers.

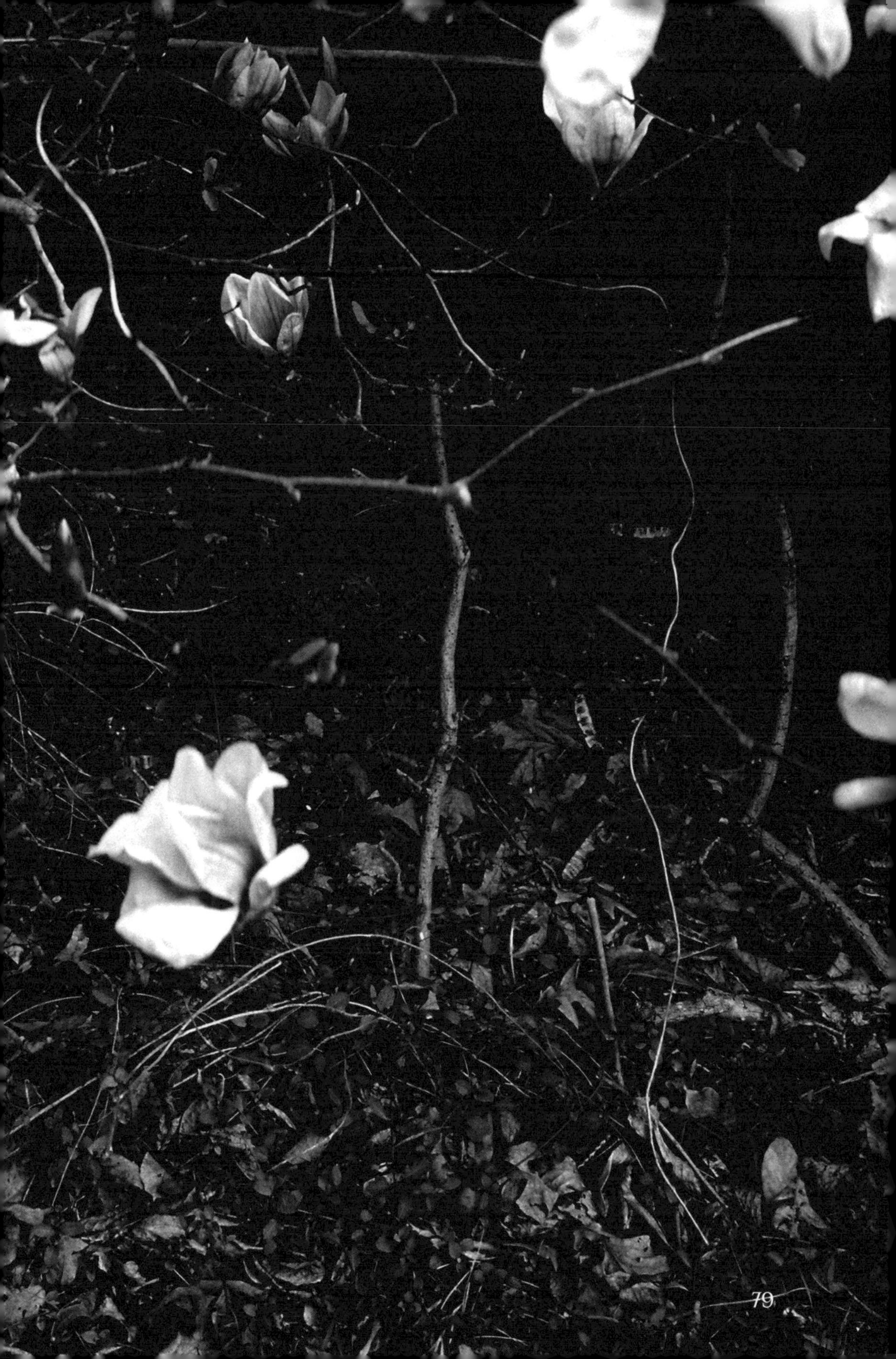

THE PARENTS

The centaur that pleads to be torn in two –

His fear revived and courage expelled, Tos'zend pleaded with the East and West to break him. The brazen hinges of the body torn, tied to the pillars of the earth. To curse the names of my father and mother as the pieces of me refuse to find one another. His mother, queen, raised wandering eyes from the temples, around her the world had blown away. And stopped weeping at the feet of the stallion.

Raised by the warrior's frame and heart of wickedness, wailed in grief to the North and South: Take pity on the claim of my parents. Trembling. Burning. Let me quit the field of play. An empty picture feeding the mind of the child, despair renewed like a chariot aflame. The white sails that took them far from humanity was an immortal betrayal. The sword which disconnects the cruel, imbued with that which defies our desires.

Blood inscribing the procession of time and histories now mine. Standing unmoved by my helpless hand, now extended to the reaches of the earth for salvation.

TIGER MOUTH

Two white rabbits with four eyes each race across the fields of wheat of mortal planters. They are chased by the god of the hunt, Ladrih, the one with ears that can hear the dawn of the universe. They are chased ten thousand times around the galaxy and hide in the mouth of the sleeping tiger. Their eight eyes quivering on the wet warm tongue of the beast, safe in the jaws of love.

The tiger wakes and shakes his head, king of deception, keeping his hidden ones from Ladrih's eye. Now the three are lovers, the rabbits that race around the field and the tiger who takes the young in the town. The tiger opens his great mouth and the rabbits kiss every fang. They sleep in peace from the hunt. When the people of the town come to find the tiger, the rabbits run across their feet, leading them away on a run across the world.

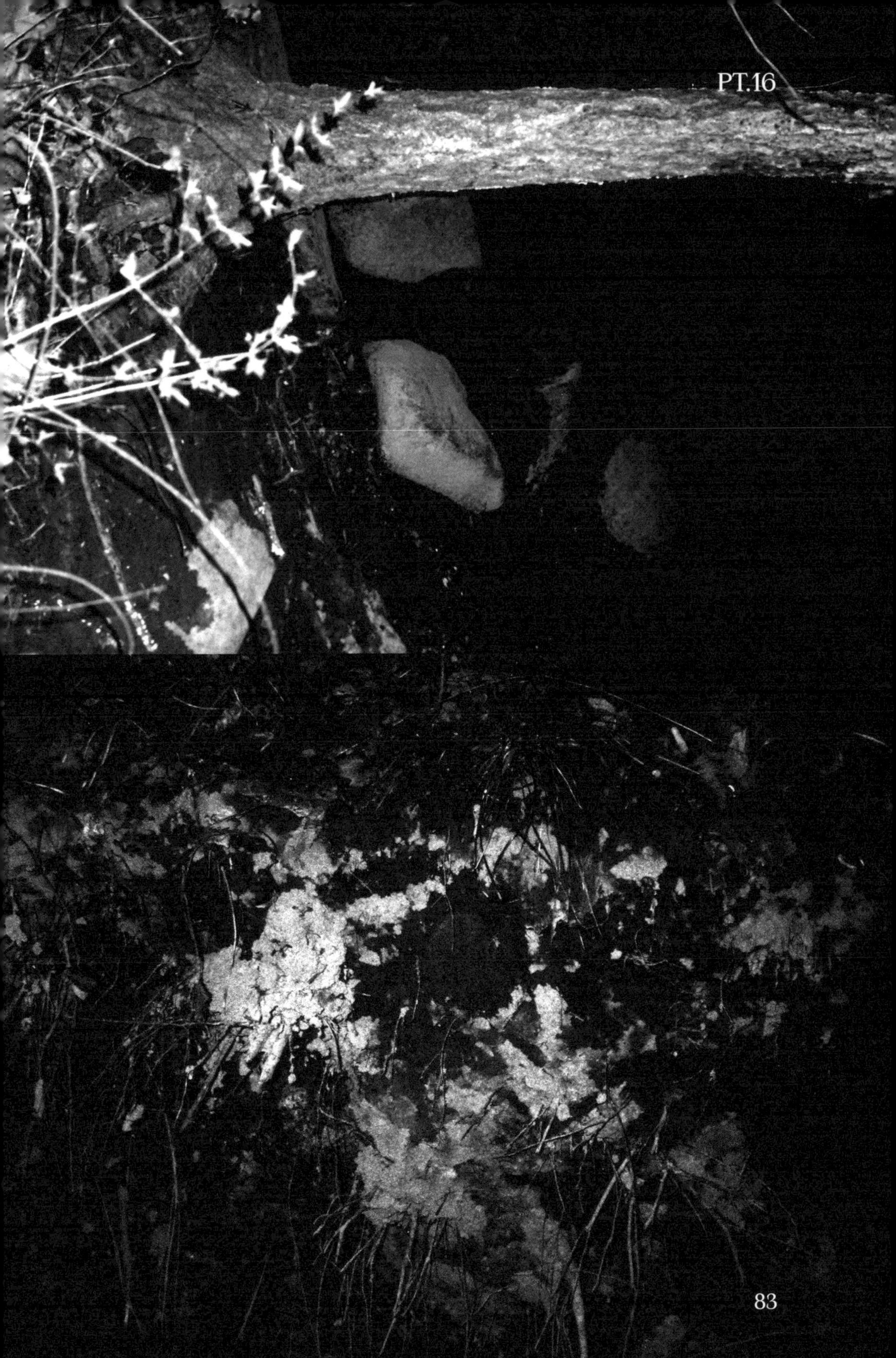
PT.16

LOT

Semele, who brought forth the forces of eternity through some fell necromancy: from the corpse of her father, she created the mountains and trees. From his spine came forth the icy peaks, his lips the rolling fields. His eyes were plucked out by the twin ravens that sit on Semele's shoulders, always watching the fates of the world. His blood grew the crops, soaked into the soil. His calves were eaten by the wolves of the world. From his eyelashes, great spears were made and given to the armies of Hera. Amidst the press of the earth for more, she refuted it, now graceful godless lands. The liver offered up to the sun and she reaches down and feasts. So she charms the heavens. The ravens watch as the birds and animals of the wood cast lots and throw dice for the teeth of the mighty god.

The goblins, who owned the earth when it was just magma and stone, dance to the flutes Semele gave them, made of the finger bones. They play songs that make the animals walk on two legs and jump over holy fire. Man lay with the beast and the angels came down from the heavens, prompted by their song, and shed their clothes. Their wings dripped with milk and honey. And from each rib, the original feral gods were born: Sokro, Bacchus, Viglath, Atshal, Saltus, Viafen, Argal, Vunnardas, Xua, Jilde, Qamuc, and Mirtinah.

And once all lots were cast, the boar and the falcon took their winnings, drunk off the starlight wine of men, and Semele faded into dust for her desires had been completed.

BLACK SWAN

In the later days, the sunset left the sky and was shrouded in brilliance. All bowed before them, unable to stand before their magnificence. They walked the morning woods for the first time, with their back pressed to the morning dew, they watched the sunrise, humbled by xeir softness. The tempest of the heart tossed them and they ached for their touch. With joyful haste, they joined hands and all in heaven for a moment held their breath. And day and night folded together and the sky burst forth, time was broken and none questioned it. Their kiss was painted with the lowly voice of the sunset.

The days reeled and the old became young again and trees died and rivers ran dry and rains came – thus, Viafen consulted with the council of Semele on the order of time. Two dryads came forth and offered up their spirits to carry the morning and night, and the sunrise and sunset laid down and were soaked into the earth. From where they had lain together, the fruit trees of the mortal world burst forth.

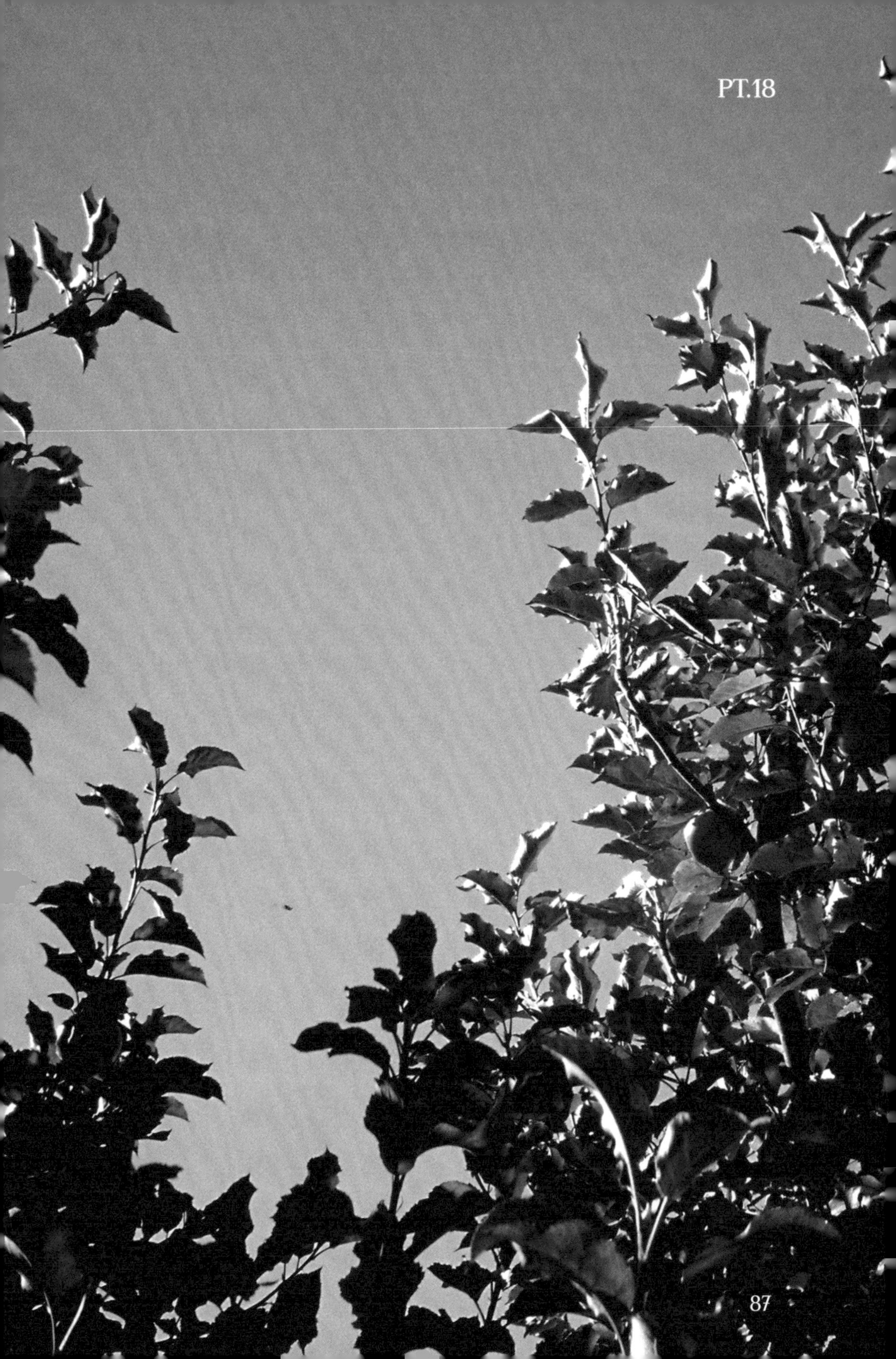

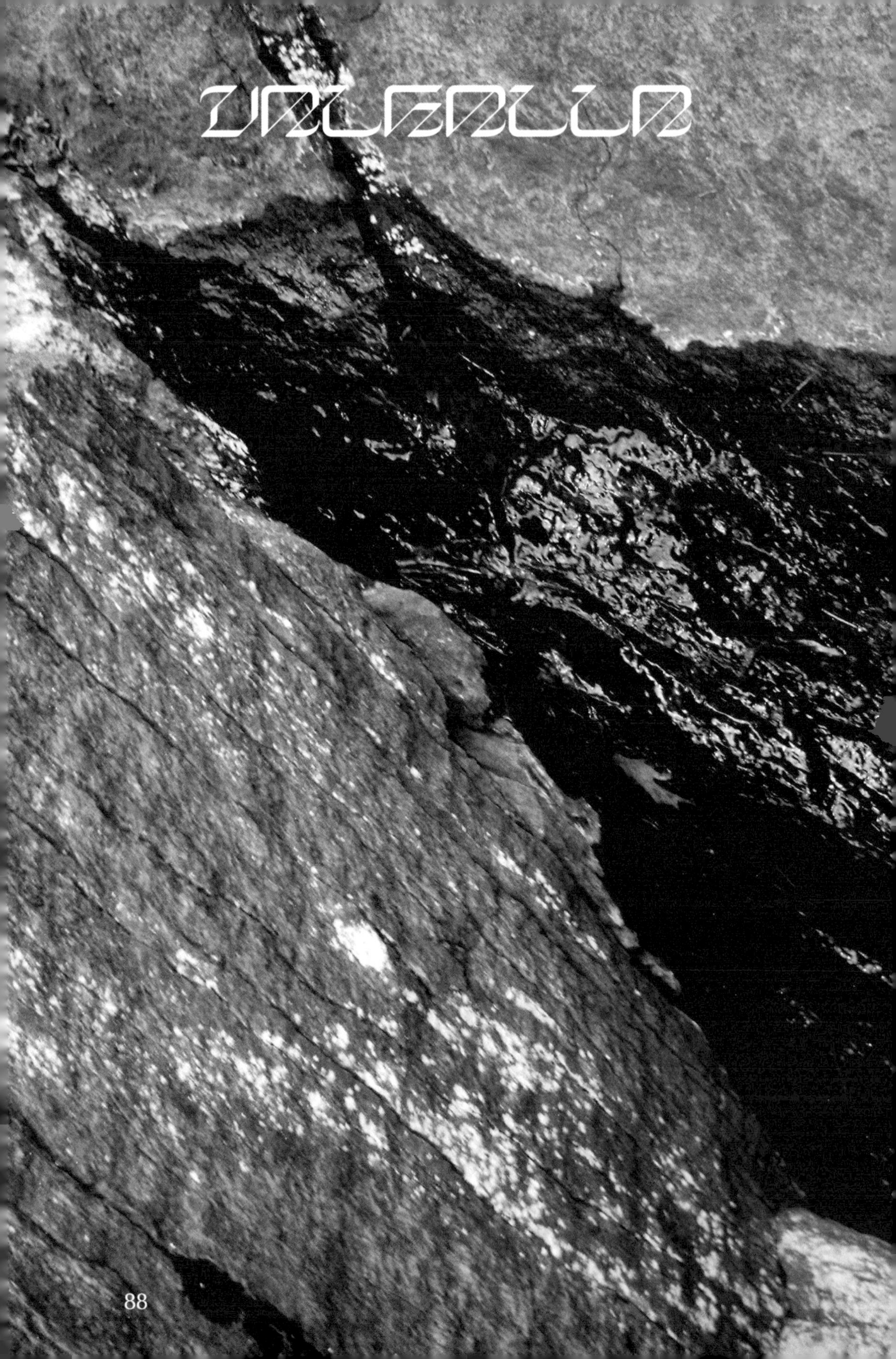

VALHALLA

The wild inhibitions that were tossed to the shore. What washed up was the armor of my brothers and the swords of my lovers and the ocean runs red. We come not with the designs of wasteful prey like the poets told, but we come with little hope or desire for the fallen. The soil of this place is fruitful, soaked with the slain, and the roots of the crabapple tree are deep though planted so soon. The weary eat their fruit, and wounds sew shut from its precious nectar.

Into her halls, not as fugitives of grace, but in tenderness, I kiss the brow of my brother, the one who left our family when I was young. It is in the arms of my eldest brother I am lifted out of the pit, the Wyvern rider of the east. And when he falls in battle, he comes back in the floods that wash our bones out to sea.

And in break of the morning, our jawbone as clean as pearls,
inspected by the gods

A spear in the side of the pegasus

The shield shattered by the sound of the earth's wailing

I kiss the knuckles of my brother, each one cold as the peaks.
Two fingers in the mouth of the sovereign
A chalice filled with the waters of youth

Before speech there was touch
Before me there was him
Before cruel fate we were destined to find our way here
Before doubt there was heaven.

1000 LIVERS

Seoningsin was desired by many in heaven. Their arms were strong, their eyes filled with fire and they were a great poet among the mortal kingdoms. Ekvir, one who was called the mightiest of torments, took the form of a great wolf and chased Seoningsin through the woods until they collapsed from exhaustion. As Ekvir forced his embrace upon Seoningsin, they bit out the god's throat, tearing out his vocal chords. Other gods and mortals said on that day (which all call the Voiceless Wolfblood Moon), they could feel the universe tremble with the soundless screams of Ekvir. The vengeful god then cursed Seoningsin to wander earth as a nine-tailed fox demon for 1000 years and if they did not eat the livers of 1000 men, or get one man to pledge them their eternal love without voice, then they would be banished to hell.

Ekvir then took Seoningsin's tongue and crawled back to the hole from which he came. The other gods watched quietly, unable to stop Ekvir from exacting such injustice. Seoningsin could shed no tears. They wandered for years unable to find love. Hundreds of years passed and mortals forgot the injustice done to them and spread myths of their monstrosity. Seoningsin could be seen kneeling in the woods, their silk gown like a lamb covered in scarlet, eating the liver of their prey.

But Seoningsin's heart was empty and they longed for other human touch and pleasure and went to the temple of the feral god, Viglath, and pleaded for them to relieve them of their misery. Viglath (who was known as the parent of all dragons that inhabit the realms, loved for giving mankind music) came down to their temple and Seoningsin, wrapped in many coils around the kumiho and in the safety and privacy of the scaled god, wept. Viglath could not lift the curse, but flew to the ends of the earth to take the livers of bad men and brought them to gentle Seoningsin who ate each in the arms of Viglath.

Once all 1000 livers had been consumed, Seoningsin's curse was lifted. Viglath offered Seoningsin anything their heart could desire and Seoningsin chose to be split into two forest dragons that slumber between four pines. They act as the guardians of those who walk the woods alone, and you can hear them sing great psalms together.

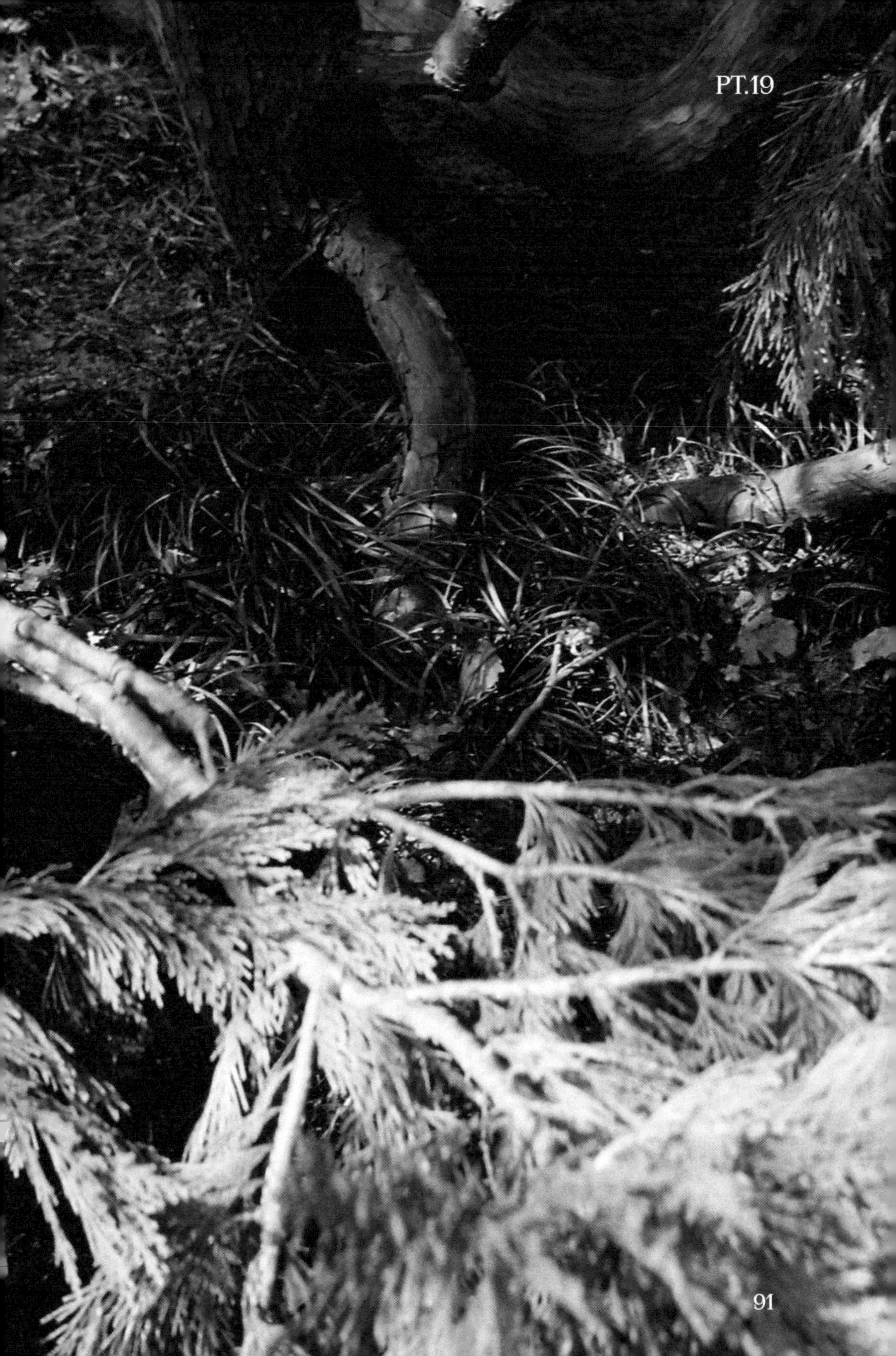

PT.19

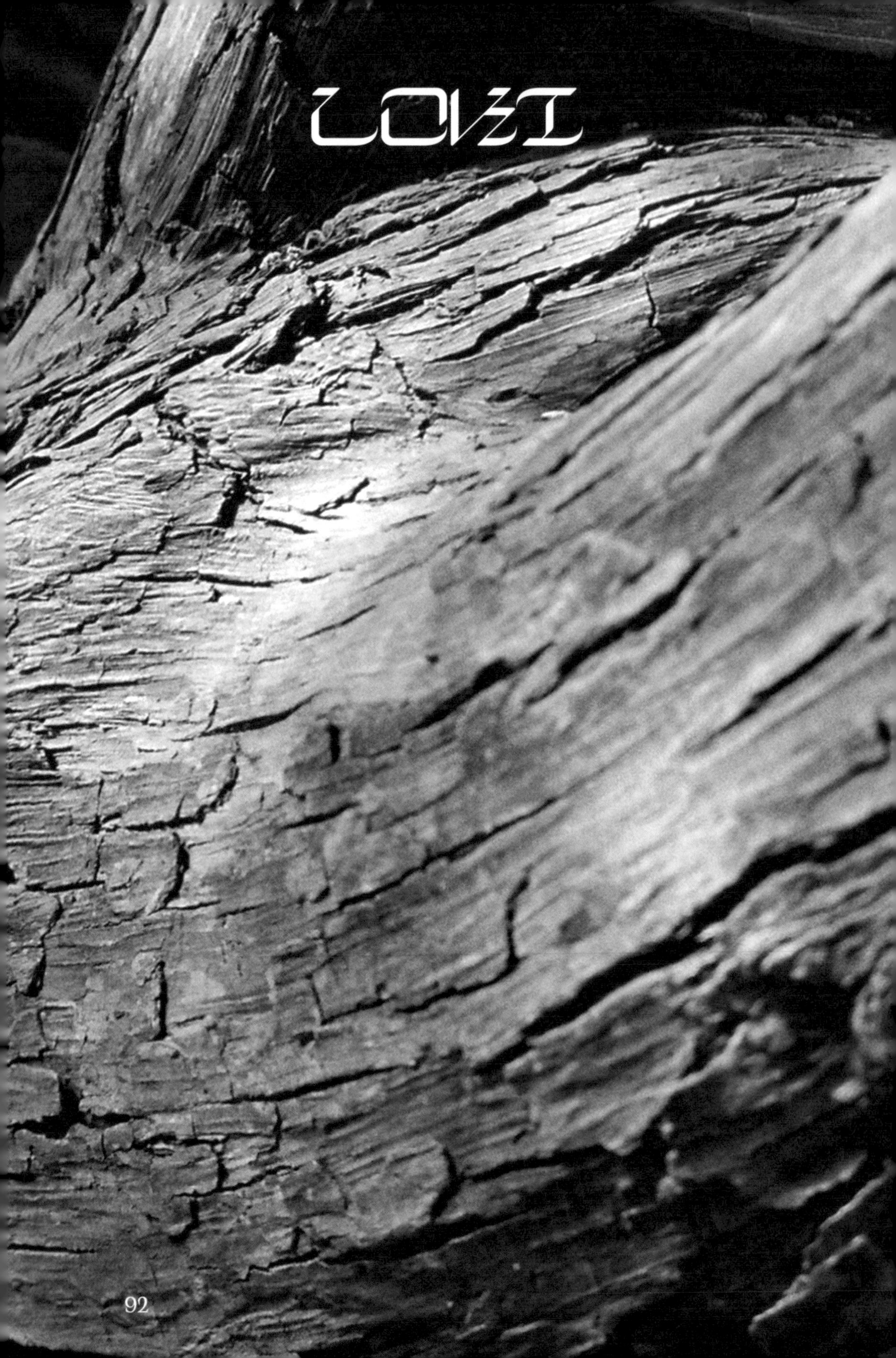
LOKI

There is a ten-sided coin used by the four-gendered prince of luck who sleeps with men who are lonely and lends ear to the heartbroken or cheated to decide the fates of those who wish to do harm. The ten-sided coin that is used by the prince of luck at the gambling and dinner table. The prince of luck who gave the jaguar its eyes, the carnivore with the biggest eyes, in a game of dice won by the jaguar. The prince of luck who abstains from all substances. The prince of luck who is also prayed to by mothers and guards the grain of the field and the hearth of the humble.

Curses his father's name

THE SPIDER

Siw-Une, the god of all things that spin and weave. The god of hair. The garment maker of all shapeshifters. Who spun the cloak of Achilles. They weave the hair of all those born into the universe.

Siw-Une resides in the eye of Jupiter and was blessed by Semele with eight hundred fingers and eight hundred hands. They are revered greatly by all in the pantheon and were born with no legs, hovering above the darkness of space combing through and kissing every thread that binds and grows.

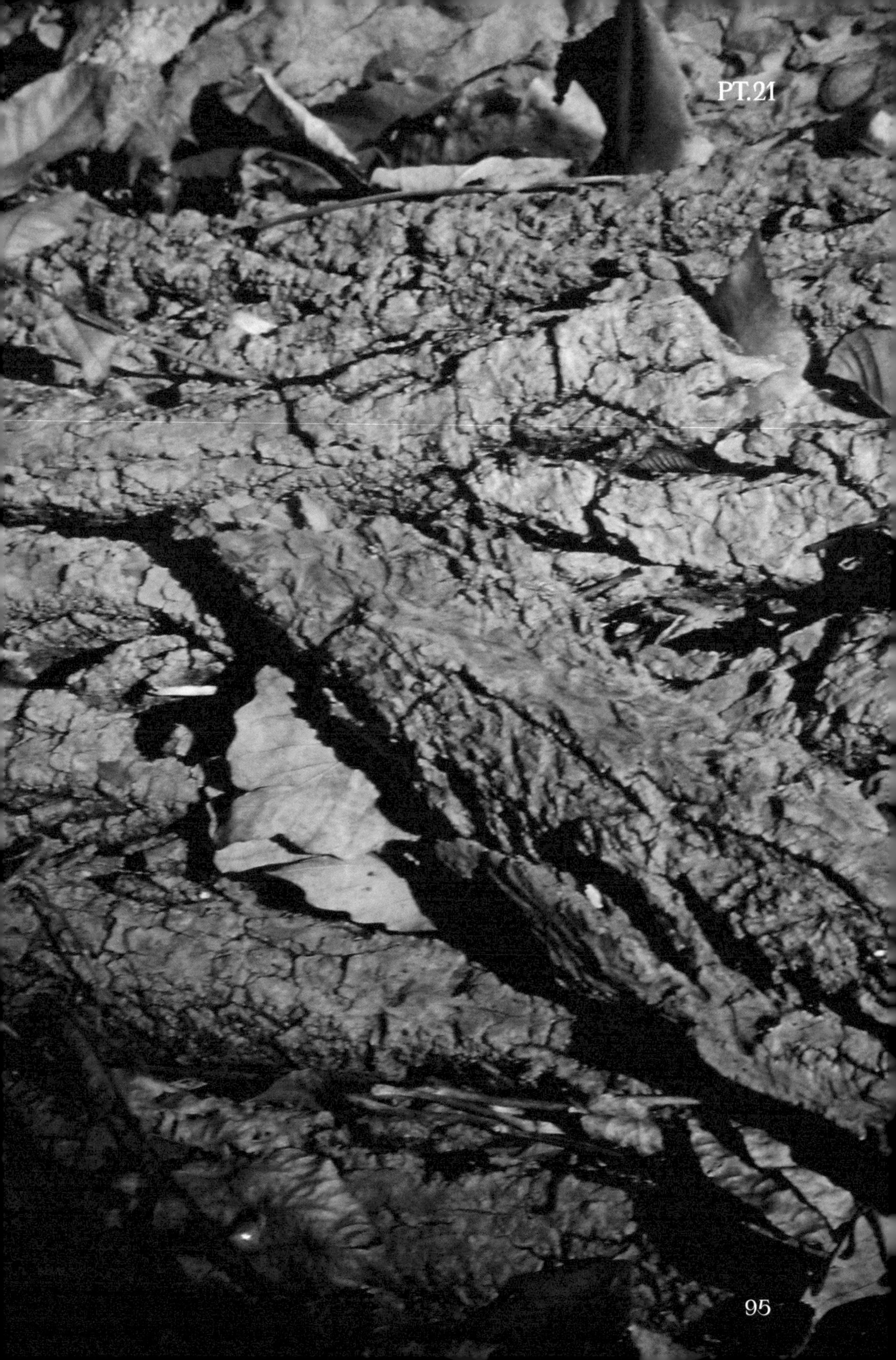
PT.21

THE MOUNTAIN

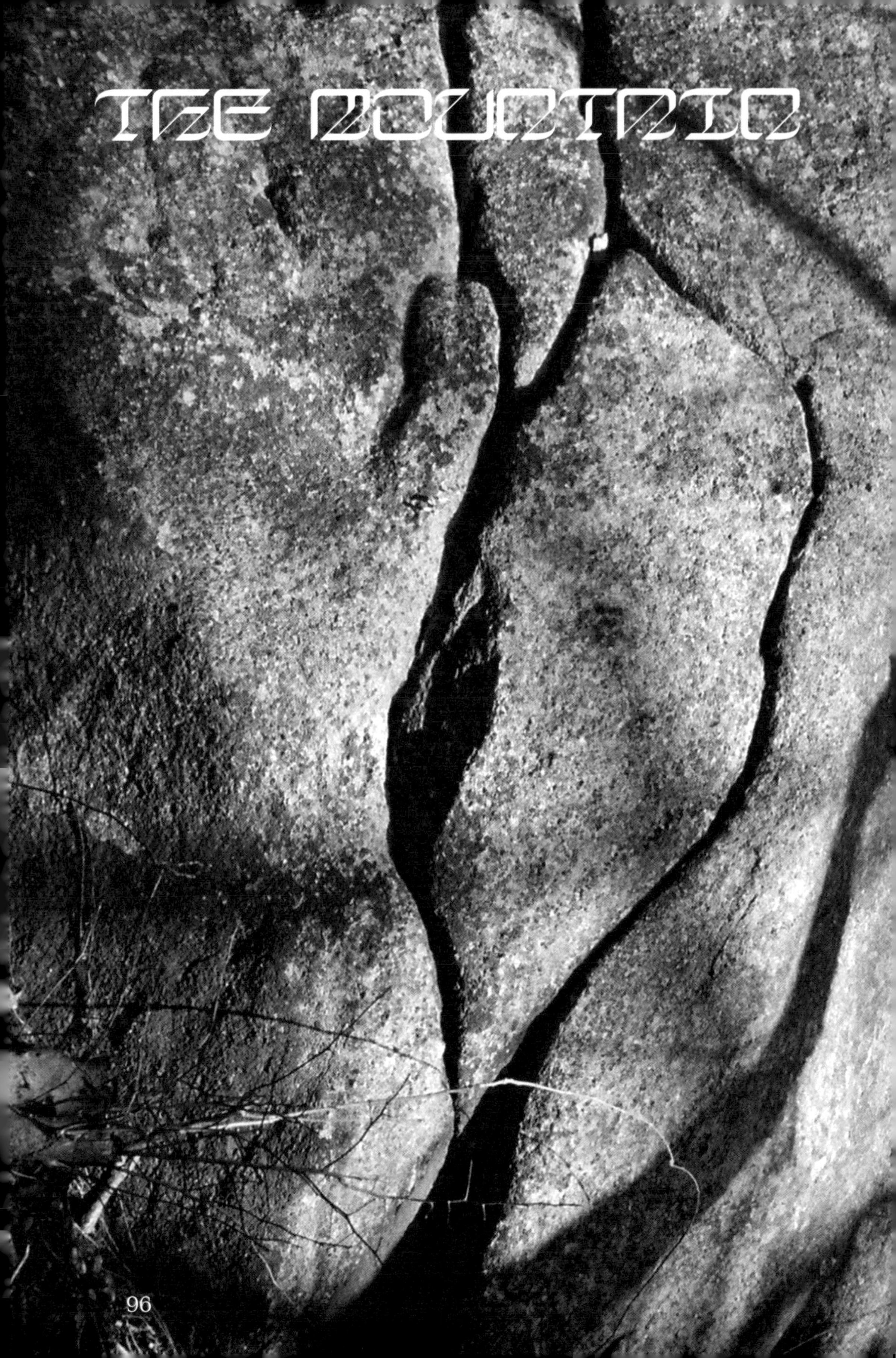

There is a mountain, Hallasan, where at the peak is a knife with a red hilt and silver blade that was placed by the elf lord of the mountain, adored by all who plow the field and forge the blade. In the old days, you could see him there eating liver and onions, drinking dark liquors with sweet nectar and telling stories to the weary and broken.

His eyes sparkled like the sunlight on the water and from his head, two great horns like that of the ox god himself. And on the mountain, those who heard him sing felt their heart light and joys many.

Soon-Jo, elf lord of the mountainside.
Of him the harpers gladly sing;
the one whose realm was fair
and free
The trees do bow and bells ring

His laugh was long, his eye was keen.
His shining eye afar was seen;
His horns did stretch beyond the sky
And hands the hammer and plow of the weary lie

But long ago he was smote down
by the plague god Makay,
The people still mourn to the
blood moon's day;
Take pilgrimage to his knife
if they can,
To honor the gentle lord of Hallasan

THREE WIVES

The doe eating from the palm of the war god's hands. They want not fire, but are the great chaos that leaps from the hearts of men. Not violence but feeling – what makes a war but opposing desires and the power to crush out the opposition? Are not games war? Is offering the stag water in cupped palms and the chance that they may drink not war? The war god wants true war, not violence. Not humans' warped wars of vengeance.

The war god holds all innocent in their arms and finds those who harm them unjustly. The curved scimitar of Ila held in the two left hands of the war god. Ila who prevents unjust battles. Ila who protects the hearts of those who are willing to fight for peace. Ila the war god, who is married to Yesfaen, the empress of peace, whose six arms hold the scales of the galaxy, who has no nose or lips but seven ears down her spine. The war god Ila who is married to Yesfaen who are both married to the princess of healing, Gifvyre, the horned one, who is called ten thousand names and exists through the hearts of all those who yearn on earth.

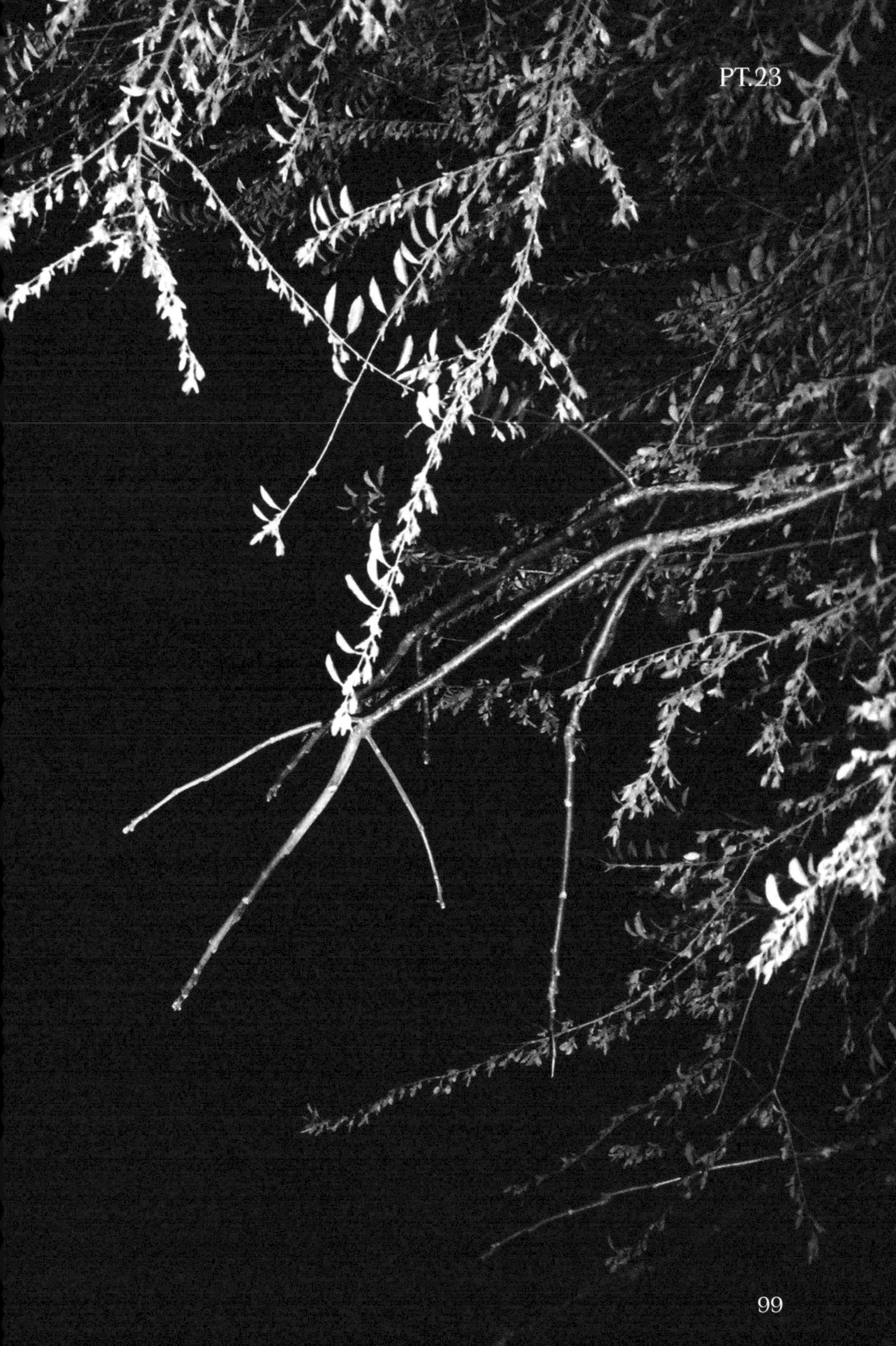
PT.23

PERSIMMON

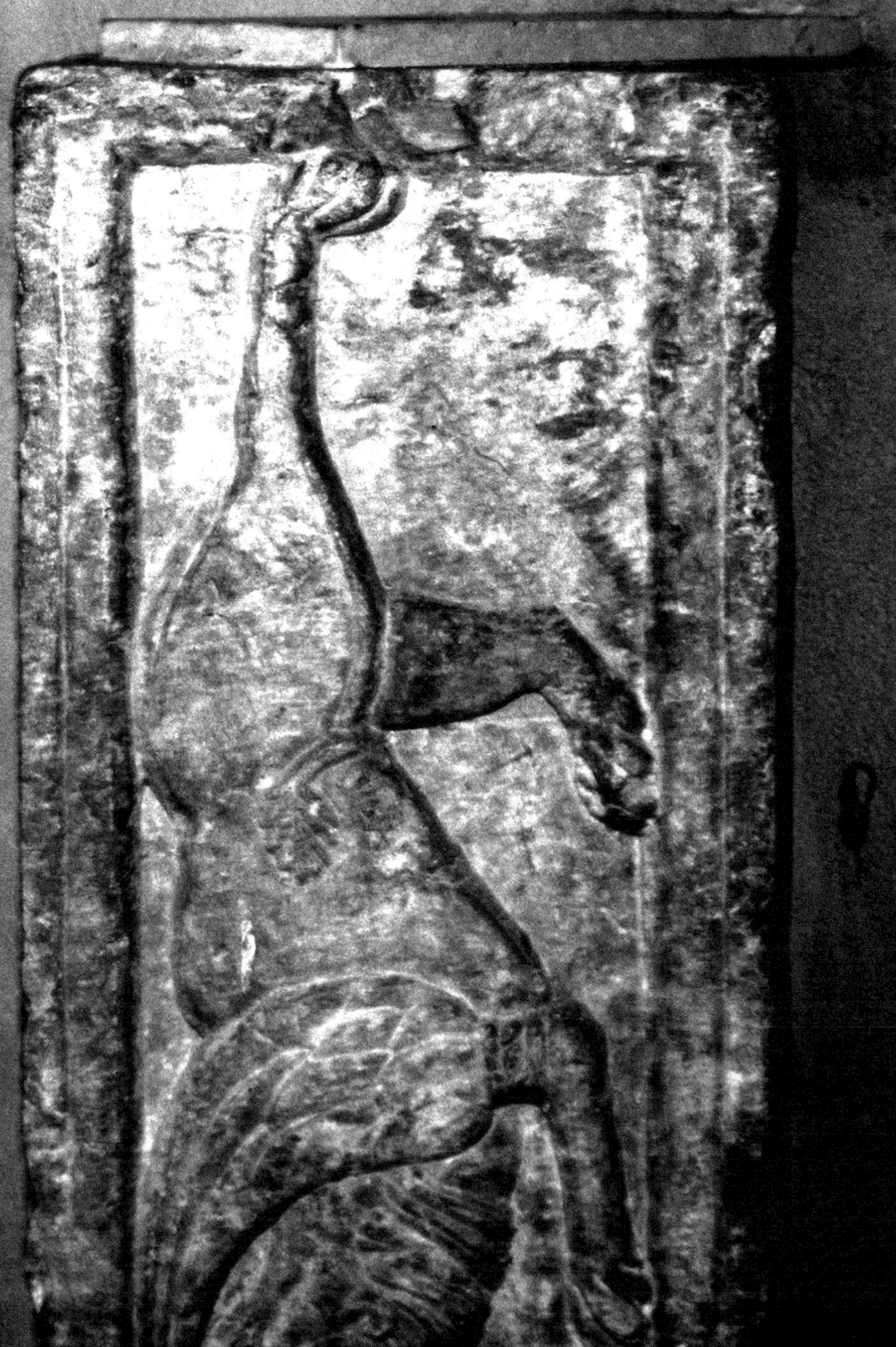

From the scripts of Ellingol in the great library the poet writes:

WHY DO THE MYTHS OF MY PEOPLE END IN TRAGEDY (THE PERSIMMONS ARE STRONGER THAN TIGERS) A TIGER HAND COVERED IN FLOUR / MY MOTHER'S HAND IS THE HAND OF A TIGER / MY MOTHER RIPS OUT THE BELLY OF THE TIGER AND EATS HIS FLESH RAW ON THE KITCHEN FLOOR AND MY BROTHER AND I CRY WATCHING AND SHE ASKS US WHAT WE HAVE TO CRY ABOUT. SHE MAKES US SHIN RAMEN AND I CANNOT TELL IF IT IS THE HAND OF MY MOTHER OR THE HAND OF THE TIGER.

She grows soft with age. Her sentiments are ripe with tenderness – but still I do not trust it. I wonder if all those years ago the tiger ate my mother and has been raising me this whole time. I wonder if the whole time my mother has been a tiger. I inspect my skin daily and see faint stripes running along my back and know in my heart the latter is true.

The tiger is cunning and beautiful. Seduces the hunter and has children with fiery volatile tiger blood. They must fulfill their duties to their patron god Xua, feral lord of cunning, and protect all liars and thieves.

THE GARDENER

Chu'shi'ien and Vlkiri, the twin planets that orbit the sun (when they were still apart), would shine their glimmering auras down upon the tomb of Mehu, the ghost that tends to the flowers that are trampled or plucked before or in bloom.

In the celestial light of the planets, they emerge from the jade tomb in which their body was placed by Soo Val, when an arrow passed through their heart wrongly in heaven's last war. In the garden, beyond mortal sight, grows an infinite field that one could call paradise in eternal bloom. Untouchable. Unharmable.

> Tender with the gentle grace of one long freed from the affliction of greed. The blood of the fallen in wars stretching to the end of time waters its orchards. Never allowing life to be lost, but regrown in the depths and richness of the earth. The marrow of kings crushed to dust and buried with the rose bulbs.

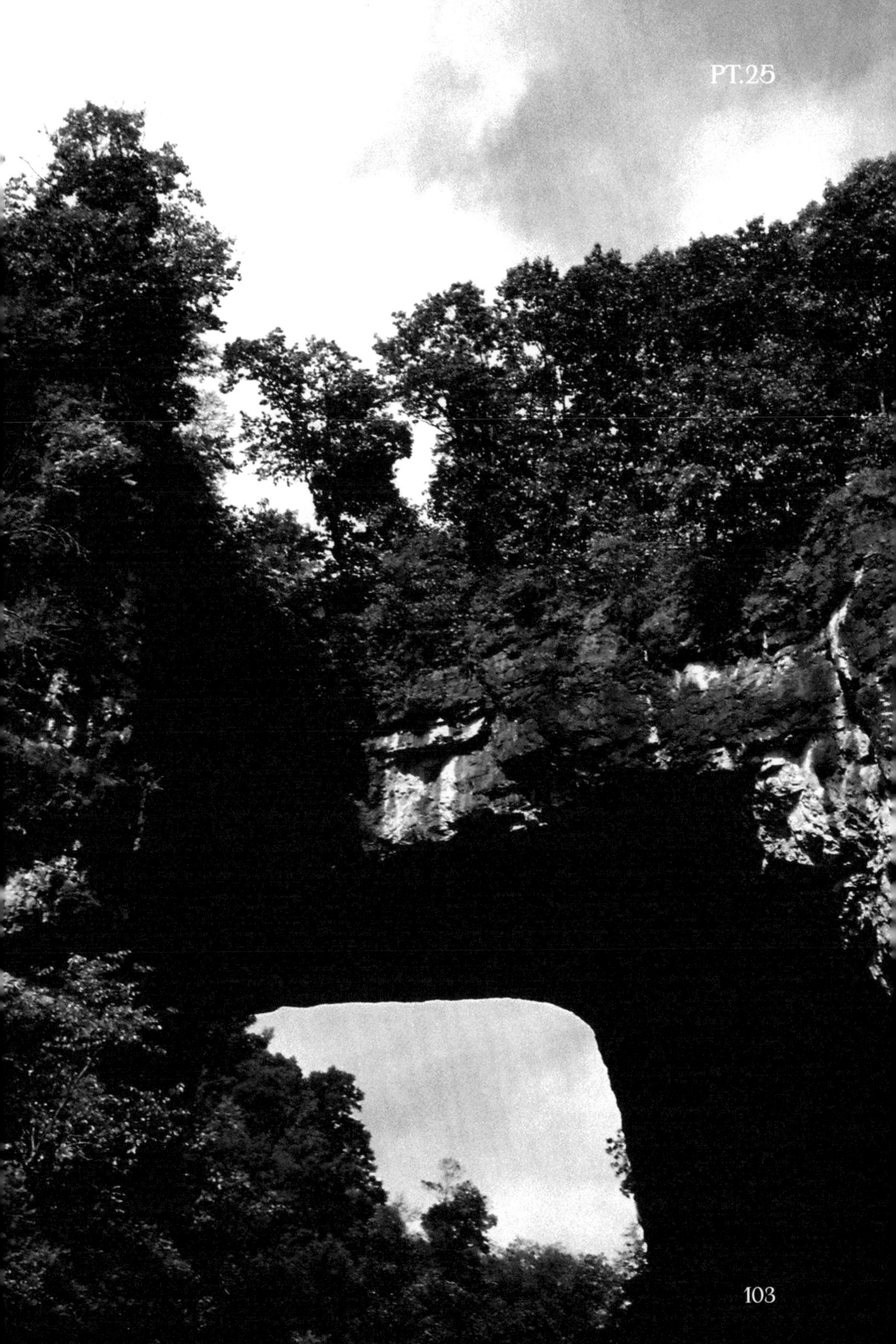

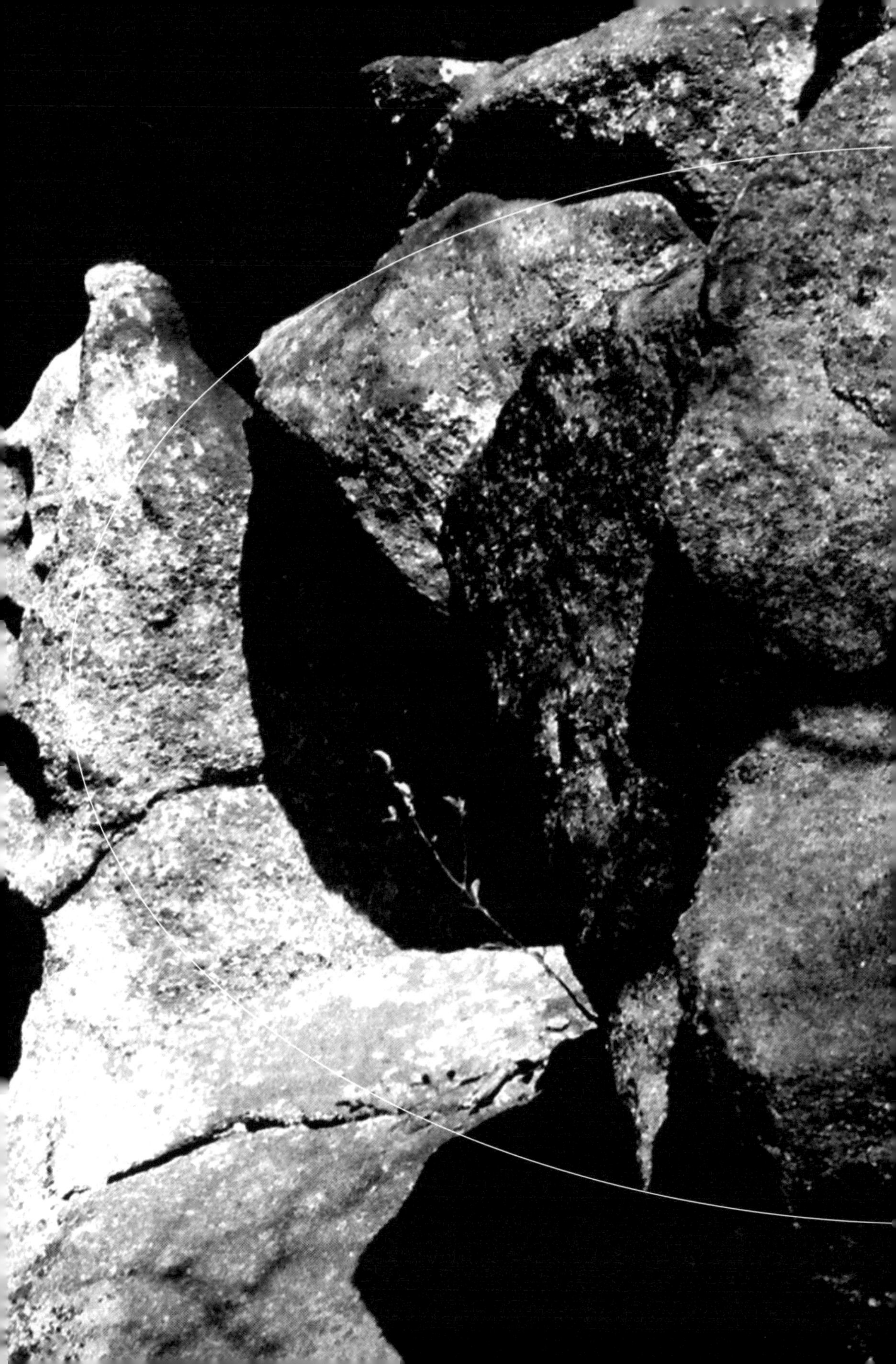

ANOINTED WITH ECSTACY

Hunters Follow Harpy Shadows
Rin Kim

Published by Printed Matter, Inc.

First edition of 1000 copies
ISBN: 978-0-89439-100-2

Design: Rin Kim
Photography: Oliver Davis
Editing: Olivia Ross
Production: The Uses of Literacy

Typeset in Arachne by Leonhard Laupichler, Apoc by Matthieu Salvaggio and Ilya Ruderman and Mughal by Jose Houdini and Fabio Florez

Printed and bound by die Keure, Belgium

Printed Matter, Inc.

Printed Matter, Inc.
231 11th Avenue
New York, NY 10001
www.printedmatter.org

Published as part of Printed Matter's Emerging Artists Publication Series

This publication is made possible with the support of the Jerome Foundation, The Andy Warhol Foundation for the Visual Arts, public funds from the New York City Department of Cultural Affairs in partnership with the City Council, as well as the New York State Council on the Arts with the support of Governor Andrew M. Cuomo and the New York State Legislature.

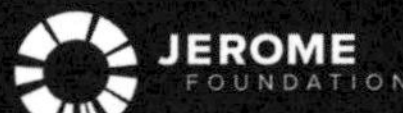

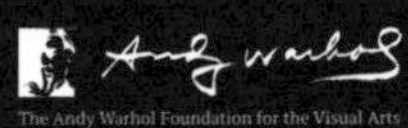

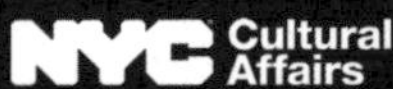

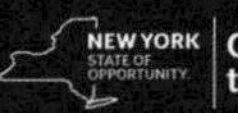